This book describes over 200 species of wild flower, all of which you can see in Britain. Identification hints are given for each flower — size, colour and so on — together with details on where and when to look. The introduction is full of helpful information and advice on flower structures, fieldwork and how to keep a record.

The book has been designed as a practical spotter's guide. Flowers are illustrated on the page on which they are described and/or in the colour pages (see index). To assist recognition, the flowers in this book are grouped within six typical habitats.

About the author

Tony Hopkins grew up in Derby in the 1950s and '60s. He was inspired by writers and artists like Eric Ennion and Peter Scott into keeping notes and diaries, and drawing whatever he saw on hitch-hiking trips around the country. Subsequently, his commitment to environmental education has carried him through teaching, the National History Museum in London, the Wildfowl Trust and a field studies centre. He now works for the Northumberland National Park where he is responsible for visitor services and interpretation. He has written and illustrated several books, and, like most other naturalists, has a very tolerant wife and understanding family.

ACKNOWLEDGEMENTS

Even a modest little book like this takes a lot of putting together. The author wishes to thank everyone who helped, from Ian Sampson who recommended the excellent artist Andrew Hutchinson, to John Richards who read the text and was a mine of useful advice. Most of all, he wishes to acknowledge the tremendous support, and hard work, of his wife Mary who approached the project with a rare blend of enthusiasm and common sense.

The publishers gratefully acknowledge Tony Hopkins and Nature Photographers Ltd for the use of their photographs. All photographs by Tony Hopkins other than those on the following pages, supplied by Nature Photographers Ltd.
23, 41, 44, 53 (Hawkweed), 56, 63, 69, 72, 74, 77, 81, 83, 84, 90, 92, 95, 96, 97, 102.

Glovebox Guide

WILD FLOWERS OF BRITAIN

Tony Hopkins

Produced by the Publishing Division
of The Automobile Association

4

Editor: *Roger Thomas*
Art Editor: *Harry Williams, FCSD*
Illustrations: *Andrew Hutchinson*
Cover illustration: *Leslie Sternberg*
Typesetting: *Afal, Cardiff*
Printing: *Purnell Book Production Ltd, a member of the BPCC Group*

Produced by the Publishing Division of
The Automobile Association

Distributed in the United Kingdom by the
Publishing Division of The Automobile
Association, Fanum House, Basingstoke,
Hampshire RG21 2EA

The contents of this publication are believed
correct at the time of printing. Nevertheless, the
Publishers cannot accept responsibility for errors
or omissions, nor for changes to details given.

ISBN 0 86145 685 8

Published by The Automobile Association

Glovebox Guide

WILD FLOWERS OF BRITAIN

Contents

Introduction 6
  Using this Book 6
  Technical Terms 8
  The Purpose of Flowers 8
  Fieldwork 9
  Keeping a Record 10

Woods and Hedges 12
Grassland and Verges 33
Heath, Moor and Mountain 55
River, Lake and Marsh 71
Coast 91
Urban Wasteland and Gardens 101

Further Reading, Societies to Join 117
Glossary 118
Index 119

Wild flowers have always been important, the basis of crops and medicine and an inspiration to poets and artists. For centuries children have made daisy chains and poppy ladies, picked four-leaved clovers and held buttercups under each other's chins. Dock leaves were rubbed on nettle stings, cleavers were thrown on clothes and dandelion clocks were blown to tell the time. Today we still notice wild flowers more than we realise. They are a link with the natural world. Coltsfoot along the road verge tells us that spring is close at hand, clumps of ox-eye daisy brighten dual carriageways and help us to relax after a busy day. When flowers disappear from the countryside we become concerned about the health of our environment. Our grandparents recall with nostalgia the days when fields and woods were full of colour and there seemed to be simple pleasures to enjoy; all this without necessarily knowing the difference between figwort and fat hen.

This book includes over 200 common flowers of the British countryside. Each species is illustrated either in black-and-white or in colour, and the text includes descriptions linked with snippets of information about each flower's ecology, history and traditions. The total complement of flowering plants in Britain is about 1,700. This includes many obscure species unlikely to be encountered or noticed on casual visits to the countryside. However, any selection designed to make identification easier is bound to involve the omission of some interesting and attractive plants. If you find a flower that does not appear in this book, look on page 117 where there are suggestions for further reading.

USING THIS BOOK

To simplify its use in the field the book is divided into six major groups of habitats comprising woods and hedges; grassland and verges; heath, moor and mountain; river, lake and marsh; coast; and urban wasteland and gardens. Although it is convenient to group plants into such habitats, the real-life situation is never so clearly defined. Vegetation comes and goes. There may be woodland species lingering in a field long after the trees have been felled, or mountain species which find comparable conditions on coastal cliffs or on church walls. The most common or characteristic plants of each habitat have been included in the text, sometimes with additional less abundant but very eye-catching species. Grouping them under habitats is practical; to do so by their scientific classification would make the text difficult to use without prior knowledge. Within each habitat group, flower species are arranged in their scientific order.

Flowering plants are separated into families, and like human families they vary. Some contain a large number of look-alike species, others have only a few distant relatives, dissimilar in features and hard to pick out in a crowd. The biggest families are the grasses and the sedges, neither of which is included in this book, but the *Compositae* (daisy family) is very large as are the *Cruciferae* (cabbage family), the *Umbelliferae* (carrot family) and the *Leguminosae* (pea family). Other families, such as the *Labiatae* (dead-nettles) and *Violaceae* (violets and pansies) are rather smaller, and some, like the *Hippuridaceae* (mare's-tail family) have only a single British representative.

Below: *Selfheal*
Right: *Bulbous buttercup*

Each species carries a scientific or Latinised name as well as its common name; this helps us to be precise about its identity. 'Cow parsley' is used for several quite different plants around the country, but its Latinised title *Anthriscus sylvestris* only applies to one species and is part of an international system of nomenclature. This does not mean that scientific names cannot change as more is learned about classification, but the objective is to arrive at a standardised list of names usable throughout the world. (see 'A note about names', page 117, for further information).

The individual name follows a binomial system comprising generic and specific parts, rather like a surname being followed by a christian name. The individual's name provides clues to its relationship with other species; in a book of this size such complexities are hardly apparent but it is certainly worth looking at scientific names and noting associations and even what the Latin might mean (*sylvestris* indicating woods, *arvensis* fields etc).

Plants approach survival and reproduction in many different ways and have evolved along different lines to produce a startling range of form and structure. There is no universal answer to cope with the problem of the British winter. Some plants are perennial and long lived, flowering each year, with food stored in their stems and complex root systems. They are able to 'hibernate' for the winter and withstand frosts. Other perennials are less robust and appear to die away, yet have food reserves and rootstocks, tubers, or creeping stems and are able to grow again when conditions improve in the spring. Some plants are biennial, growing from seed and developing a food reserve in one season then flowering and dying in the second year. A large number of smaller plants, especially colonisers of bare ground, are annuals completing their whole life-cycle in only a few months.

TECHNICAL TERMS

Technical terms have been kept to an absolute minimum in the text and appear in the glossary on pages 118/119. There are hundreds of botanical phrases to describe leaf shape and flower structure. Some are useful and some are not; the word 'obdiplostemonous' refers to a certain arrangement of stamens but it is not a helpful expression if you have only just discovered what a stamen is in the first place. The enjoyable early stage of getting to know flowers should not rely on such clumsy, if precise, language.

THE PURPOSE OF FLOWERS

The flower is often the most impressive and beautiful part of a plant. Its purpose is to effect reproduction, to bring about a meeting between the male and female cells. This is usually carried out with the assistance of an external agent, the wind or insects. In wind-pollinated flowers such as plantain, pollen (the male sex cell) is blown from the nodding anthers of one plant and dispersed widely over the countryside. The law of averages dictates that some pollen will land on the stigma of another plantain flower. One pollen grain will germinate and grow a tube which enters the ovary via the style to fertilise an egg in an ovule. The ovary will develop into the fruit, the ovule into the seed. In insect-pollinated flowers the anthers, carried on stamens, dab pollen on to an insect attracted by nectar. If the plant is lucky the insect will continue its search for sweet nectar or pollen

to another ripe flower on another plant and will brush against a stigma which is sticky and will pick up the pollen grains. This is a more efficient method than wind pollination but still has a random element; bees, the most important pollinators of all, visit a lot of flowers and are constantly brushing off pollen or collecting it for their own purposes.

Flowers have to compete for the attention of pollinators, hence their shape and colours and their profusion. The individual structures vary from family to family and species to species. Some examples will illustrate the principles (see illustrations).

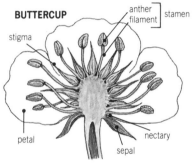

BUTTERCUP

stigma · anther · filament · stamen · petal · sepal · nectary

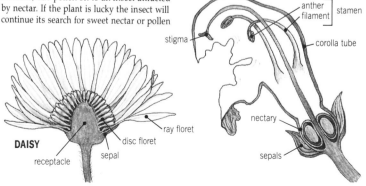

DEAD-NETTLE

stigma · anther · filament · stamen · corolla tube · nectary · sepals

DAISY

receptacle · sepal · disc floret · ray floret

FIELDWORK

Delve into the recesses of a school biology cupboard and you will probably find a vasculum, a metal collecting flask. At one time the only way to take flowers seriously was to dig them up and carry them back to the lab in such a container. There they would be pressed and dried to demonstrate details of the root, stem, leaf, flower and fruit, and taped into an album or herbarium. As collecting gave way to 'science' so the school vasculum gave way to quadrats and transects,

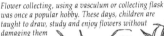

Flower collecting, using a vasculum or collecting flask was once a popular hobby. These days, children are taught to draw, study and enjoy flowers without damaging them

used in simple ecological surveys to demonstrate the interactions of plant communities and the effects of such factors as shade and soil. A quadrat is created by a simple square frame; placed on the ground, it allows a standard area to be sampled to estimate the percentage cover of plants. Interesting vegetation 'maps' can be produced. A transect is made from a line, marked at regular intervals and stretched across a survey area. The closest plant to each mark is noted, resulting in a standardised method for recording frequency.

Obviously these simple, very visual techniques still have great attraction in school biology labs. But the real ecological work has become much more sophisticated. Botany, like all other sciences, has evolved into a serious business of statistics and university research.

This is not necessarily a bad thing, for it has released the majority of naturalists from the obligation of being scientists. Flowers should be fun for most people. But a scientific approach, however modest, can add a new dimension to the appreciation of flowers, but enhance rather than diminish the magic of the subject. There is still a place for the vasculum, though these days a polythene bag suffices to bring specimens back home. It is illegal now to uproot wild plants without permission but there is nothing wrong with picking a few very common flowers to remind yourself of what they look like and to form the basis of a simple reference collection. Quadrat surveys of a back lawn over a period of a few years will answer the vexed question of whether the plantain is really taking the place over. A computer programme will allow you to analyse population dynamics. All the techniques are available, if you wish to try them.

Many people have turned to alternative ways of enjoying flowers out of doors. There are two aspects to this. The first is to combine individual skills of identification with the social side of conservation fieldwork, by taking part in local and national surveys and projects. The second is to make a series of unique personal statements by producing photographs, drawings and notes. A mixture of both approaches brings the best of both worlds to flower appreciation.

either deadly dull or tremendously exciting. It depends on what you find.

Relaying your information to your BSBI County Recorder will make you part of a network and put you in touch with other fieldworkers. You will have all sorts of unsolved identification riddles, but by now you will be able to narrow down your options, and compare notes with friends and ask for guidance on 'critical' species from local experts. When a derelict canal or coppice

Produce a list of the flowers in your garden and it will almost certainly be longer than you expected. It will also contain a few names with question marks alongside — things that you are not quite sure about. Sorting out identification by following clues, by using reference books and following keys, is very satisfying. Once the garden holds no fears then a few metres of hedgerow or river bank should keep you busy for a while. Before too long, and without realising it, you will have become an expert on your own 'patch' and the local natural history society or local nature conservation trust will be interested in your records. What were notebook reminders have become database references. National surveys, often organised through the BSBI (see page 117), are carried out by noting the presence or absence of species in grid squares of a map; fieldwork of this kind led to the classic *Atlas of the British Flora* and the distribution maps found in some modern handbooks. The updating of this information, by visiting unrecorded areas (an exercise known as 'square-bashing'), can be

Two ways to capture the beauty of wild flowers: illustration and (next page) photography

is earmarked for redevelopment, it is possible that your information will contribute to its survival. Better still, your knowledge about the state of plant communities in such places might lead to a proper management of the site by a conservation trust, so that you can become actively involved by cleaning out ponds or pulling up sycamore seedlings from an oakwood. The reward for your efforts will be to see a change for the better, the creation of a place for nature in a busy world.

KEEPING A RECORD

Keeping your own personal account of what you see is of tremendous importance, not just as a scientific record but as a memento. In future years any scraps of notes you took on a special day will be among your most treasured possessions because they will be unrepeatable. If you make your field notes or drawings on the spot they will be your immediate response to what you see and will be unique. Getting into this habit is hard work but it will pay dividends. Use a good quality unlined notebook with a hard cover. Learn to write things down as they happen, to include details that will later help you to recall the excitment of the event. Draw what you see and only what you see. Even if you have never been an artist you might surprise yourself and will certainly improve your observation skills. Use coloured crayons, biros or watercolours, whatever you feel most comfortable with.

A camera can be a blessing or otherwise. It can capture complex and beautiful images for you or make you a lazy collector of pictures. In general, it is best to be cautious; use photography to augment rather than to replace your notebook. Experiment with film; try black-and-white, colour print and colour transparency, all of which have their qualities and uses. Use different makes of film, which have quite different colour tones. A single-lens reflex camera is almost essential to any wildlife photographer. If you don't have one, borrow one while you are saving up to buy your own. You need to be able to see what you are taking and need to make judgements about shutter speed and depth of field. A moderately priced single-lens reflex will allow you to do these things. A fully automatic SLR is a waste of money as it actually restricts your options. It is a much better idea to put any extra funds into the purchase of a better quality lens which will make the difference between achieving sharp rather than fuzzy pictures.

In flower-photography strong sunshine is usually a nuisance. The contrast between the brightness of the flowers and shiny leaves and the blackness of the shadows and undergrowth is so great that the emulsion on the film cannot cope. The result is a confusing picture bearing little resemblance to what you were looking at when you pressed the shutter. A hazy bright day is very much better, certainly for classic compositions, though bear in mind that any rule is only applied so that it can be broken; some of the finest and most dramatic flower photographs are taken against the light and into the sun.

It is only when you start taking photographs of flowers that you realise there is no such thing as a still day. The wind is a constant menace and vibration will spoil the sharpness of your pictures. A tripod removes the problem of camera shake allowing you to shoot at slower speeds or with more depth of field, though there will be tiring days when you will regret having to carry one. Special models such as the Benbo tripod allow you to work at ground level — much the best angle from which to shoot flowers.

Finally, always keep the welfare of the plant in mind. Whilst you are drawing, photographing, measuring and studying your subject it is remarkably easy to trample on it or neighbouring plants. Flowers are such fun that they should be left for everyone to enjoy.

WOODS AND HEDGES

*B*ritain was once covered with trees, and surviving fragments of this original 'wildwood' often provide the most exciting habitats for wild flowers. Places that have had thousands of years in which to develop plant communities are likely to be richer than recently established areas, but this does not mean that the best woods are untouched or forgotten. In fact regular management, the cropping of mature standard trees and the cutting or coppicing of underwood, increases the light reaching the herb layer and benefits the flowers. Also, ancient woodland often appears in unlikely places, not always in extensive blocks but in tiny scraps in field corners, on steep banks and as farm shelter belts.

In the south of England the pedunculate oak is the dominant native tree, providing a classic wildlife habitat on clay soils. But there are some fascinating beechwoods too, mainly on chalk, and on the limestone hills in the west and north Midlands there are some fine ashwoods. In the north, sessile oakwoods fill many steep gorges, and in Scotland there are superb birch and pine forests. All of these different types of woodland

have their own special beauty. More recent mixed plantations should not be dismissed; there will always be something of interest. Even the dullest conifer plantations, with their rows of shadowy spruce trees destined to be clear felled and pulped, may actually have been planted over the remains of an ancient wood and be full of flowers along forest rides and clearings.

In many ways hedges are little more than linear woods and have most of the flowers that thrive in clearings. Some hedges are actually the remnants of long-vanished blocks of wildwood, or were planted in Anglo-Saxon times so that they are of historic as well as botanic interest.

Woodland flowers can tolerate some shade but respond well to sunlight, so rides, pathways and clearings are the best places to look when the canopy is closed and the forest floor is in shadow. Spring or 'vernal' species avoid the problem by flowering before the trees are in leaf, carpeting the ground for two or three weeks and producing one of the most magical sights of the British countryside.

WOOD ANEMONE *Anemone nemorosa*

Wood anemone is a flower of the early spring, carpeting many old woods but especially abundant in places where coppicing is still practised. It also occurs in pastures and on mountain slopes. The anemone gets its name from the Greek *anemos* meaning wind, and it is still known as the windflower in many parts of the country. The flower, about 3cm in diameter, is composed of 5, 6 or more sepals,

white in colour but tinged purple/pink. These radiate out from a bunch of yellow stamens with a core of green carpels. The leaves are deeply forked, a group of three half-way up the flower stem with other groups, springing from roots or rhizomes, appearing nearby.

The effect of coming upon a glittering sea of anemones in an otherwise wintry and leafless wood is breathtaking. In cloudy or dull weather the flowers half close and nod, but in sunshine they open fully, extending the plant to a height from 5—30cm. The flowers are virtually scentless (but give them a try — according to Geoffrey Grigson they are supposed to smell 'rather unpleasant . . . yet . . . intriguing'). They produce no nectar and are pollinated by bees and wasps intent on stealing pollen.

GOLDILOCKS *Ranunculus auricomus*

This is a woodland buttercup, found especially on fertile lowland soils. The plant is a perennial growing from a rootstock and has a very variable set of leaves. The lowest are round or kidney shaped, but the majority are deeply lobed. The flowers are about half the size of those of other buttercups and are much less numerous. Even when dominating a woodland glade in spring or early summer, goldilocks does so with restraint. Many flowers have some reduced or deformed petals, contributing to the plant's untidy, leggy appearance.

The name 'Goldilocks' is often used locally for other buttercups, including marsh marigold and globe flower, and also for a yellow aster.

Goldilocks with detail of flower head

LESSER CELANDINE *Ranunculus ficaria*
Celandines are a familiar sign of early spring in open woods, shady meadows and river banks. The flowers, 2 or 3cm in diameter, have three green sepals and a variable number (between 7 and 12) of shiny yellow petals which bleach white after a few days of March sunshine. The leaves grow from a rosette and are long stalked, broad and glossy green. Lesser celandine is a perennial, appearing year after year in the same place, growing from root tubers and sometimes from bulbils, which, through a belief in 'sympathetic magic', were used in medieval medical treatment and earned the plant the name 'pilewort'.

COMMON DOG VIOLET *Viola riviniana*
This is the common violet of woods and pastures throughout Britain, but there are several similar species, especially in the south. Violets are perennial herbs, growing from rootstocks to a height of 10 or 20cm. The leaves are heart shaped and deep green. Most have purple-mauve flowers, about 2cm in width, which appear in March and April. The flowers are unusually shaped having uneven petals. The spur at the back of the lower petal

identifies the species — the common dog violet has a pale broad spur whilst that of the early or **pale dog violet**, *V. reichenbachiana*, is dark and tapering. One species, the **sweet violet**, *V. odorata*, has a strong scent and has been widely planted in gardens and hedgerows well away from its natural range in the south and east.

RED CAMPION *Silene dioica*
The deep rose-pink petals of red campion brighten wood edges and verges from April to October. The flowers measure about 2cm across and have five deeply notched petals. Close examination reveals that they are not all the same; those on some plants have 10 stamens whilst those on others have five well-developed styles. The former are male, the latter female. Individual plants produce flowers of a single sex.

This is a shade-tolerant biennial or perennial plant but in extreme gloomy conditions it tends to grow tall (nearly a metre high), pale and with fewer flowers. The leaves are opposite, broad at the base but narrow further up the stem. The whole plant is covered with soft hairs. The papery capsules, which persist long after the tiny black seeds have been dispersed, are useful for winter flower decorations.

JACK-BY-THE-HEDGE *Alliaria petiolata*
Many plants have alternative names which
are now quite obsolete, but this species has
retained its touch of old familiarity. It is
known as garlic mustard or hedge garlic in
some modern books, but 'Jack-by-the-hedge'
reflects an age in which the plant grew
abundantly beside dusty tracks and farm
gates. It is still a very common plant, a
biennial or a perennial growing from bulbils,

easily recognised by its tall erect stem up to a
metre high. It has broad, heart-shaped leaves,
fresh salad-green and welcome as a sign of
spring. When lightly bruised, they give off a
mild smell of garlic and are supposed to be
very good in sandwiches or as an alternative
to mint sauce.

The flowers, like many other crucifers,
are small (up to 6mm across) and four-
petalled, white in colour and giving way to
long thin seed pods. Looking among the
flowers in May it is usually possible to find
the bright-orange, skittle-shaped eggs of the
orange-tip butterfly laid upon the new pods.

WOOD SORREL *Oxalis acetosella*
The shamrock- or clover-shaped leaves of
wood sorrel bring a vivid green to shaded
woods. Dense patches spring from a network
of creeping rhizomes, growing out of moss, in
leaf litter or on rotting stumps. In normal
daylight the leaves open fully but at night, or
when the sky is too dull or too bright, they
fold neatly back onto their stems. The flowers
are out in April and May. They are five
petalled and white with violet veins, and
grow on thread-like stems to a height of up
to 10cm.

The leaves have a sharp, fresh and not
unattractive taste, but the oxalic acid that
imparts this flavour is poisonous and an
overdose of the plant has proved fatal to
sheep. It was once cultivated for use in salads
and probably did no harm when taken in
moderation. Its most precious attribute
today is to lighten the deep gloom of
coniferous plantations.

Wood sorrel

GREATER STITCHWORT *Stellaria holostea*
Picking stitchwort is supposed to provoke
thunderstorms and it was, as the name
suggests, used as a remedy for sharp stabbing
pains. There is no scientific evidence to
support either belief!

Greater stitchwort is a perennial and
grows from a creeping rootstock to a height of
between 20 and 60cm. The stems are thin,
square (or rectangular) and brittle, and tend
to lean on other woodland vegetation to gain

some protection from the wind and rain. The
leaves are thin, rough edged and taper to a
fine point, giving the whole plant a grassy
quality. The flowers appear from April to
June. They are very attractive, up to 30mm
across and composed of five white petals
each deeply notched or divided to
approximately half its length.

HERB ROBERT *Geranium robertianum*
Perhaps its habit of growing among the
shadows of old gardens and forgotten
woodland tracks has led to the long
association of this innocuous plant with the
darker side of country life. The name
probably has its roots in Robin Goodfellow, a
mischievous fairy who was always close at
hand to tip over the milk pail or unlatch the
chicken coup.

Herb Robert is an annual, sometimes
persisting over winter into a second year,
growing to a height of about 40cm. The leaves
are attractive, composed of five leaflets deeply
fingered and notched, giving the foliage a
lace-like quality. Often the whole plant is
bright red — leaves, stems and all. The
flowers, appearing throughout the summer,
are five petalled and 15—20mm across, pink
with red veins. As with other members of the
crane's-bill family the seeds develop in long
'beaked' fruits.

Herb Robert

TUFTED VETCH *Vicia cracca*
Vetches, and their close relatives tares, are members of the pea family but they have finely fingered or pinnate leaves, often separated into a dozen or more leaflets.

Tufted vetch is probably the most noticeable species, having a scrambling stem up to 2m long, branched tendrils curled like coiled springs around any possible support, and dense flower heads of up to 40 blue/purple flowers. These are out from June to August, after which a cluster of pods develops, each pod containing up to six seeds.

Tufted vetch is a perennial, overwintering as a rootstock, and is found at the edges of woods and along hedgerows and roadside verges.

If left uncut, most brambles grow into scrambling, impenetrable bushes up to 3m in height. The flowers grow in panicles on the tips of the previous year's stems. They are white or pale pink and, along woodland rides, are the most important nectar source for midsummer butterflies. The black 'berry' is in fact a tight cluster of 'druplets', fleshy fruits like miniature plums or cherries, inside which are cased seeds ('pips'!).

Blackberry picking is a prickly business

BLACKBERRY *Rubus fruticosus*
Blackberries are a mid-autumn harvest. They are produced at a time when foliage is turning orange or red, hence it is useful to have black fruits which birds, the main agent of dispersal, can see clearly. There are dozens of different kinds of brambles making up an aggregate or grouping of over 300 separate 'micro-species'. They vary in choice of habitat, prickliness of the thorns and the taste of the berries. All but the most eccentric amateur botanists leave the task of identification to the experts.

HERB BENNET *Geum urbanum*

The leaves of herb Bennet (also known as wood avens) are composed of small lateral leaflets but with a much larger lobed leaflet at the tip. Once known and recognised, it is often the foliage that is picked out first along damp wood edges and rides where the species is most common.

Although the plant grows up to 60cm high, the flowers are quite small, appearing singly on long stalks and measuring about 1.5cm across. They are composed of five pointed green sepals above which, and alternating with the sepals, are five rather small pointed petals, bright yellow in colour. After flowering from June to August, a head of nutlets or achenes develops; these are hooked and rely for their dispersal on passing badgers and foxes, or by wandering cats which then return home and preen out the seeds on to carpets and sofas. Years ago, the clove-smelling rootstock of this perennial herb was used to keep moths out of linen.

WILD STRAWBERRY *Fragaria vesca*

Fruits of the wild strawberry are small and it takes a lot of disciplined collecting to have enough to fill a dessert spoon. The taste makes it worth almost any amount of trouble. The bright-red colour of strawberries is an invitation to all animals and birds, the evolutionary intention being to have the tiny seeds swallowed and excreted at a later time and place. The succulent flesh is the price the plant must pay for the service.

The wild strawberry grows from a rootstock to a height of 5—30cm and spreads by runners. The leaves grow on long stalks and are trifoliate, composed of three egg-shaped and deeply toothed leaflets, shiny green on top but silky grey underneath. The flowers are small, no more than 18mm across, and have five white petals. During the flowering season (April to June) it is easy to overlook this little plant among the rich flora of scrubby woods and pastures on basic soils. By midsummer the nodding fruits have proclaimed their presence to mice and blackbirds and the short sweet harvest is under way.

The cultivated strawberry, developed over the last 300 years, is derived from an American relative.

BARREN STRAWBERRY *Potentilla sterilis*
Superficially like wild strawberry but more
closely related to the cinquefoils, barren
strawberry does not grow a succulent fruit —
hence its common name. It is a perennial of
dry wood banks and open hedgerows,
growing from a woody rootstock to a height
of about 10cm. It often flowers very early and
is at its best in March and April. The leaves
are trifoliate, blue/green and silky. The end
tooth of the middle leaflet is short, not
projecting beyond those on either side as is
the case with the wild strawberry. The white-
petalled flowers are easy to distinguish too:
the petals of the wild strawberry are slightly
pointed and touch each other, whilst those of
the barren strawberry are notched and have
gaps through which the five green sepals
show clearly.

DOG ROSE *Rosa canina*
The flowering season of wild roses is all too
brief, usually just a few days in the middle of
summer, so it is worth stopping a car or
delaying a picnic to enjoy their fragile beauty.
    Dog rose is the biggest of the wild
roses, often growing to a height of 3m and
sending out a cascade of arching branches
over other hedgerow vegetation. The branches
are covered with curved, broad-based thorns
(some other roses, such as the lovely **downy
rose**, *R. mollis*, have long straight thorns).
The flowers grow singly and are large, up to
5cm across, with a simple rosette of pale-pink
petals. The leaves are composed of 5 or 7
leaflets and are sharply toothed.

ENCHANTER'S NIGHTSHADE
Circaea lutetiana
An imaginative name for a very unobtrusive
plant. Enchanter's nightshade is a perennial
herb, 30—70cm tall, which grows in damp
woodland on basic soils and is usually to be
found in dark and gloomy places. The leaves
grow in opposite pairs up the stem. They are
oval, tapering towards the tip, and are
slightly toothed. The flowers appear between
June and August, grow on a tall slender spike
and are rather small, consisting of two deeply
forked petals, pale pink, 3—4mm long.
    How the plant got such a romantic
name is obscure as it is totally unrelated to
the true nightshades such as deadly
nightshade and bittersweet (page 79). A
sleeping draught was once made from it. The
scientific name is *Circaea*, Circe being an
enchantress in Greek mythology.

*Enchanter's
nightshade*

SANICLE *Sanicula europaea*

Sanicle was a healing herb in medieval times: hence its name, from the Latin *sano*, I heal. It is an unusual plant, a member of the Umbellifer family, but the dense little flower heads or 'umbels', 5 or 6mm in diameter, are round rather than platform shaped, and the outer ring of individual flowers is composed of stamens only. The inner flowers are white or pink in colour and are very small; it is these that develop later in the summer into hooked seeds which are picked up in the fur of woodland animals and subsequently dispersed far and wide.

Most of the leaves, shiny and deeply forked, grow from the base of the plant on tall stalks. Sanicle is a perennial, growing up to 60cm high, flowering from May to August, but it is not a showy species and is often overlooked among communities of other woodland plants. It is found on lime-rich soils in beech and ash woodlands and also in old loamy oakwoods.

DOG'S MERCURY *Mercurialis perennis*

An old Yorkshire name for this leafy plant of dark places is 'boggart-posy', 'boggart' being a particularly nasty sort of woodland fairy. Dog's mercury grows especially well on limestone soils but will thrive in many dry shady situations, often along hedgerows linking old woods and coverts.

This is a perennial herb with long creeping rhizomes, sending up fresh green stems in the very early spring to a height of about 40cm. The leaves are opposite, broad and spear shaped and about 8cm long. They form a dense dull-green foliage which soon shades out other vernal plants such as wood anemone and primrose. The flowers are very small, no more than 5mm across, composed of green sepals rather than petals. Male and female flowers grow on separate plants, the males densely on a tall spike, the females 2 or 3 at a time on a short spike. The latter develop into hairy fruits on elongated stalks. Like its relatives the spurges, this is a poisonous plant, described by the great herbalist Gerard as 'dangerously purgative'.

Dog's mercury flower heads, male (right) and female

WHITE BRYONY *Bryonia dioica*
In an early autumn hedgerow the bright-red berries of bryony add a considerable splash of colour. The plant climbs and clings, its long stem held by coiled tendrils rising from the bases of leaf stalks. The leaves are large (usually 10—15cm in length), deeply lobed and sculpted.

Unlike the seeds, the flowers are unobtrusive, though they must be clearly visible to bees. Male flowers and female flowers grow on different plants; both are greenish, appearing from May to September. Bryony is a poisonous plant and is our only native representative of the cucumber family.

PRIMROSE *Primula vulgaris*
For over a thousand years the primrose has figured in folk songs and stories. In recent years it has become a talisman for town dwellers with their hearts in the country, but it is an increasingly scarce plant around cities where it suffers from over-picking.

The primrose is a perennial herb growing from a rhizome which in the late winter sends out a rosette of wrinkled leaves, heavily veined underneath, broadest at their tip and up to 15cm in length. The flowers follow in March and April — sometimes much earlier and sometimes continuing into June if the season is cool. They grow on pink-flushed, downy stalks from a main stem base. What look like five petals are in fact the lobes of a corolla; these contract into a narrow mouth where the cream-yellow is augmented by a streak of orange. The scent is sweet and reminiscent of violets.

YELLOW PIMPERNEL *Lysimachia nemorum*
Closely related to the ubiquitous creeping Jenny of hanging baskets and cottage gardens, this is a perennial of damp woods and hedgerows, draping itself over the leaf litter and growing to 40cm in length. The leaves are opposite, 2—4cm long, slightly fleshy and shiny green like creeping Jenny, but oval and pointed rather than rounded.

The flowers are warm yellow, a corolla with five calyx teeth, opening to a diameter of 10 or 12mm. The flowers grow from leaf axils on very fine stalks, usually only 2 or 3 at any one time, so the plant rarely puts on a great show. It is, however, likely to be met with at any time between May and September, in all but the driest woods.

COMMON FIGWORT *Scrophularia nodosa*
Flowers that are pollinated by wasps are often purple/brown in colour. This is certainly the case with figwort which is almost exclusively visited by these insects, the flowering season coinciding with their peak abundance in mid- to late summer.

The flowers, produced on a panicle or branched spike, are small (about a centimetre long), the corolla consisting of three green lower lobes and two purple upper lobes. These rounded upper lobes are a little larger in size and hood the open mouth of the

roots were prescribed by medieval medics who supported the doctrine of signatures ('if it looks like something it must have been put here by God to cure it'). The scientific name *Scrophularia* also comes from a signature cure, this time for the so-called King's Disease, scrofula.

Common figwort

The foxglove, purple and poisonous

FOXGLOVE *Digitalis purpurea*
Foxglove is found in several habitats but it is most at home in woodland clearings and hedgerows where the soil is dry and acidic. It is a biennial, growing a rosette of broad, spear-shaped, downy leaves. A flower spike or raceme up to 150cm tall is produced from June to September of the following year. The purple corollas are big enough to fit over a thumb or fingertip. More significantly, they will accommodate bumblebees. The lower flowers develop first; as these are pollinated and the corollas drop off the next few buds open, and so on through the summer. The stamens ripen before the stigma, so that as bees work their way up a spike and across to the lower flowers of the next plant, cross-pollination is assured.

corolla, hiding a quartet of stamens. Figwort is a perennial plant of damp woodland and hedgerows, growing to 80cm tall. The name is derived from the Latin *ficus*, meaning a haemorrhoid; the nodules and tubers of the

Foxglove is a poisonous plant containing digitalin, the original source of the heart stimulant.

WOOD FORGET-ME-NOT
Myosotis sylvatica

This is the plant from which the garden forget-me-not was developed. There are several other closely related species, though none more attractive, which have been used through the centuries as a sign of constancy.

Whilst in exile the young King Henry IV took forget-me-not for his family emblem, and the motif appeared in subsequent Plantagenet designs and decorations.

Wood forget-me-not is a downy perennial up to 40cm high, the leaves being either spoon shaped in a rosette at the base, or oval on the stem. The corolla of the flowers, up to 10mm across, is composed of five broad blue lobes radiating out from a yellow central mouth. Misty carpets of this large-flowered forget-me-not occur in most damp woods in early summer.

COMMON COW-WHEAT
Melampyrum pratense

The name is a derogatory one, referring to the apparent worthlessness of the plant and the old belief that if its seeds contaminated a corn harvest the resulting flour would turn black. Cow-wheat is an annual, and a semi-parasite, getting some of its nutrients from the roots of other plants. It is most characteristic of mixed woods on acidic soils and grows best along rides or in temporary clearings that have been created by coppicing.

The leaves are narrow and pointed, the stem simple or branching, growing to a height of 50cm but usually much less. The flowers, appearing between May and September, develop in opposite pairs from the bases of long spiky leaf bracts, but they always grow to face the same direction along the side of the stem. The individual flowers are about 15cm long, composed of a five-toothed calyx and a long, pale-yellow corolla. The mouth of the corolla is usually half-closed and the only insects powerful enough to force their way inside to collect nectar and effect pollination are bumblebees.

HEDGE WOUNDWORT *Stachys sylvatica*
A plant of woods and hedgerows on rich soils, often appearing amid a tangle of other shadowy herbs in July and August, hedge woundwort is a creeping perennial with a flower spike up to 80cm high. Like other members of the dead-nettle family the flowers are carried in tiers or whorls. They are a deep crimson or purple/red colour blotched with white, and have a narrow corolla allowing pollination by long-tongued insects such as bees and moths. The leaves are heart shaped,

up to 9cm long, toothed and extremely hairy. They have a very pungent smell when crushed or bruised, a smell often described as 'unpleasant' but so characteristic of summer that it is hard to be critical.

YELLOW ARCHANGEL
Lamiastrum galeobdolon
A lovely name for a pretty dead-nettle, found along woodland paths and glades, most commonly in the south of England on heavy soils. The leaves are 5 or 6cm long and grow in opposite pairs up the stem. They are oval, pointed and heavily serrated, growing on a tall square and hairy stem, and are narrower than those of other dead-nettles and not so nettle-like in appearance.

The flowers grow in whorls, several tiers to a stem. They are buttercup-yellow and downy, composed of a calyx and a long elegant corolla, its lower lips usually streaked with red or brown. Yellow archangel is a perennial, spreading by stolons, flowering in May and June.

GROUND-IVY *Glechoma hederacea*
This is a short, straggling or creeping plant, common along hedgerows and overgrown borders in city parks and in most kinds of woodland. The leaves are conspicuous, as in many shade-tolerant species, heart shaped, rounded at the tip and bluntly toothed. They are covered with hair and grow in pairs along a square stem.

Until the 16th century, when hops became popular, ground-ivy was used to flavour and clear ale; the leaves have an astringent or bitter smell when crushed. The flowers grow in whorls around the bases of the leaf stalks and are purple/blue; the corolla is up to 20mm long with a three-lobed lower lip. This is one of the first flowers of spring and is usually over by the end of May.

Ground-ivy

Top right: *Wood anemone*
Middle right: *Red campion*
Bottom right: *Jack-by-the-hedge*

Lesser celandine

Herb Robert

Yellow archangel

Dog rose

Barren strawberry

Primrose

Bluebell

Giant bellflower

Ramsons

Top right: *Bulbous buttercup*
Middle right: *Maiden pink*

Foxglove

Meadow crane's-bill

Silverweed

Common milkwort

Red clover

Kidney vetch

Ground-ivy

BUGLE *Ajuga reptans*
The nectar of this unassuming perennial herb is very sought after by butterflies. It has few other obvious attributes but has unusually dark leaves. These are round tipped and smooth, and can be a dusky violet in colour, especially those which shorten into bracts high up on the stem.

are more oval or spear shaped with much shorter stalks. Each stem carries a raceme of several flowers. These have corollas 4 or 5cm long, usually purple/blue but sometimes white in colour. It is the size of these tube-shaped flowers that comes as such a surprise. Giant bellflower is a perennial flowering in high summer, commoner in the north than the south and characteristic of woods and hedgerows that are very shady.

Bugle has a very dense flower head, a series of whorls each made up of 5 or 6 flowers growing from the axils of a pair of bracts. It is out from May to July. As in other dead-nettles or labiates, the stem is square and the flowers are composed of a spiky calyx and an attractively sculptured and colourful corolla. This is bright blue, heavily veined, with two small side lobes and a much larger lower lobe. Although characteristic of most kinds of woodland, especially clearings and coppices, this plant can also be found on open hillsides. It grows to a height of 10—25cm and spreads from its rootstock by means of long runners or stolons.

GIANT BELLFLOWER *Campanula latifolia*
Few wild flowers are encountered during a woodland walk that are so impressive as the giant bellflower, a goliath among a family of plants that also contains the harebell (page 69). The stems are up to a metre in height and are slightly hairy. The leaves are bluntly toothed; those growing directly from the rootstock are heart shaped, those growing alternately up the stem decrease in size and

WOODRUFF *Galium odoratum*

A plant that was once gathered and used to mask the fusty smell of stored linen, woodruff gives off a lovely fresh scent of new-mown hay when it has been recently cut. It is a member of the bedstraw family, characterised by distinct whorls of rather pointed, narrow leaves. In the case of woodruff the 'ruffs' are composed of 6—8 rough-edged leaves each up to 4cm long. The flowers are less distinctive,

ivory coloured, small (about 5mm in diameter) and funnel shaped with a four-lobed corolla, grouped together in umbrella-shaped heads. The stem is square or oblong in cross section, and grows to a height of between 15 and 30cm.

This is a perennial herb of calcareous woods, often overlooked but sometimes very common even in mature beechwoods. It is in flower during May and June.

HONEYSUCKLE *Lonicera periclymenum*

This is a climbing shrub often trailing over other bushes in an untidy sprawl, or twining (always in an anti-clockwise direction) around their stems, to a maximum height of 6m. The simple leaves of honeysuckle appear early in the year when spring is some weeks away, but the flowers do not show themselves before June. When they do they are spectacular, growing in dense terminal heads or bunches, each flower with a narrow corolla up to 5cm long, broadening into an upper and lower lip from which the anthers and stigma protrude. The outside is pink or flushed with purple, the inside starts white but turns yellow after pollination. In autumn, translucent red berries are produced.

The flowers release a heavy evening scent, startlingly rich and powerful on a still night, which attracts long-tongued hawk-moths — especially the elephant hawk.

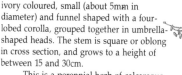

Honeysuckle (illustration and photograph)

Pollination by other insects is difficult; some bumblebees rob the flower of nectar by biting a hole in the back of the corolla tube. The frayed fibre of honeysuckle stems is a favourite nesting material of dormice.

BLUEBELL *Hyacinthoides non-scripta*
Individually, the bluebell is not especially
exciting, but in hazy oceans beneath a
woodland canopy it conjures a vision of the
British countryside at its best. Nothing like it
exists anywhere else. Bluebells grow from
bulbs to a height of 20—50cm, the stem or

scrape carrying a raceme of bell-shaped sky-
blue flowers. The flowers are made up of six
perianth segments and two blue bracts fused
at their base. They are usually at their best
between late April and late May. Proper wild
bluebells always droop slightly.

Although so characteristic of woods on
slightly acidic soils, the bluebell also grows
on grassy or bracken-covered hillsides,
especially those close to western coasts. In
times past, the slimy sap from the stem and
bulb was used as a glue, notably by arrow-
makers when attaching flights.

RAMSONS *Allium ursinum*
Few plants impress themselves on the senses
quite so emphatically as ramsons, so much so
that the name (derived from the Old English
hramsa) appears in many placenames such as
Ramsbottom and Ramsey. In suitable
situations on rich moist soils, the plant
produces a dense, deep-green carpet,
completely covering the woodland floor. It
has a pungent garlic scent, too heavy to have

gained it a place of affection in the country
kitchen, though much of its strength is
removed on cooking.

Ramsons is a member of the lily family
and like the bluebell it grows from a bulb.
Two or three broad pointed leaves, on long
twisted stalks, grow from this bulb to a height
of about 20cm, and from April to June a tall
triangular flower spike is produced. At first
the flower head is enclosed in a papery
sheath; this then bursts to release a cluster of
up to 20 white spiky flowers. The sight of a
million starry flower spikes set in a vivid
green sea is very impressive.

WILD DAFFODIL *Narcissus pseudonarcissus*
It came as a surprise to Wordsworth to find daffodils on the shores of Ullswater, but these days it is possible to find patches of cultivated daffodils almost anywhere. The wild variety is not a very common plant now, occurring in a few woods and pastures in most English counties. Where it is found in a natural state it is usually abundant, a riot of nodding heads. Wild daffodils are delicate and short

stemmed (up to 35cm high), the flowers finely formed with the perianth or outer scales distinctly paler and more straw coloured than the trumpet-shaped central tube.

The daffodil is a perennial, growing from a bulb, flowering from March to April depending on the location. The leaves are strap like, grey-green in colour and up to 30cm long.

LORDS AND LADIES *Arum maculatum*
Clumps of the broad triangular or arrow-shaped leaves of lords and ladies, often spotted with black or purple, appear in the early spring in woods and shady hedgerows. The flowers follow in April and May. Lords and ladies is known by a bewildering number of local names, many of bawdy origin: cuckoo-pint is probably the most widespread and respectable.

The flower head or inflorescence takes the form of a cluster of female flowers topped by a sequence of male flowers. These are comparatively small, encased in a cylindrical chamber, but this chamber opens out into a large cowl or hood called a spathe. Within the spathe is a purple rod called a spadix. When the plant is ripe the spadix heats up and gives off a scent, slight and not very pleasant, which attracts owl midges. These tiny insects crawl down past a ring of bristles into the floral chamber. If they carry pollen from another plant they pollinate the female flowers, whereupon the bristles wither and the midges are able to escape, picking up fresh pollen from the male flowers on the way out.

When the spadix and the spathe have shrivelled away the ovules develop into a cluster of orange berries, attractive but poisonous. Lords and ladies is a perennial, growing from a fleshy rootstock. In Elizabethan times this rootstock was crushed to produce starch used to stiffen collars.

Lords and ladies and its cluster of poisonous berries

GRASSLAND AND VERGES

G reen fields have been an important part of the British countryside ever since Stone Age farmers first cut a swathe through the 'wildwood' to provide grazing for their domestic animals. By their very nature such places are temporary; left to their own devices all but the bleakest areas would quickly revert to woodland.

For many centuries the systems of managing grassland encouraged wild flowers, but recently a move to higher, more consistent yields of grass has led to a widespread decrease of flower-filled meadows and pastures. Silage-making, where the crop of green grass is cut long before any other plants have a chance to flower, has replaced hay-making. Most open pastures are 'improved' by reseeding and the application of fertilisers, and are stocked to their capacity. Wild flowers cannot compete. This means that to find fields full of flowers it is necessary to search for marginal land where modern farming technology is impractical or uneconomic. Surprisingly, the flowers are still there to be found. There are many hay meadows in isolated valleys through the British uplands, and there are impressive south-facing slopes on the chalk downs of southern England. Less spectacular but more widespread, roadside verges are becoming an important refuge for plants of open grassland, and most parks and gardens have forgotten corners where sprinklings of colourful flowers defy the mowing machines each summer.

MEADOW BUTTERCUP *Ranunculus acris*
'Buttercup' is a vague name for almost any yellow-flowered *Ranunculus*. Once, 'crowfoot' was a more widespread name but this is now applied to aquatic, white-flowered members of the family (see common water crowfoot, page 72). The herbalist Culpepper called the buttercup a 'furious biting Herb', referring to its ability to cause blisters, both external and internal. All species are poisonous to man and beast, yet at one time it was rubbed over cows' udders to increase the yield and butterfat content of the milk.

The meadow buttercup is the commonest species of buttercup in damp fields and pastures which are regularly mown. It grows from a creeping rootstock and has no runners or stolons. In June, buttercup meadows are a joy to walk through, the plant growing almost a metre high and with a profusion of rich yellow flowers. These are composed of five shiny petals close beneath which are a ring of five hairy sepals. The flower stalks are smooth and the leaves variable — those growing from the base are long stalked and broad in outline but deeply lobed and toothed, those growing high on the stems are thin and even edged.

BULBOUS BUTTERCUP
Ranunculus bulbosus
On old 'ridge and furrow' fields turned into pastures and meadows, this flower will often be found growing at the top of the ridge where the soil is dry and shallow whilst the meadow buttercup will be growing in the wetter furrows. It flowers a little earlier in the year too, and is usually over by late May.

At a distance it can be told from its close relatives the meadow and creeping buttercups by this preference for drier, hillier ground, by its 'close-cropped' appearance (it has a shorter stem, 15—40cm) and by the cooler yellow of its flowers. To be certain, look closer, at the upper stem which is furrowed and the sepals which are turned back sharply against the stalk. The stem base is swollen into a tuber, hence the plant's common and scientific names. The leaves are three lobed, with a long-stalked middle lobe.

PERFORATE ST JOHN'S WORT
Hypericum perforatum
This is the commonest species of St John's wort, especially on basic soils. It is a tall, straight herb between 30 and 90cm high, flowering from June to September.

The stem is smooth but with a raised ridge on either side, best detected by touch. The leaves are opposite, each pair alternating in direction up the stem, and are covered by glandular dots which are translucent and give the leaf a perforated appearance, as if covered by pin-holes, when held up to the light. The flowers are smoky golden-yellow, five petalled, dotted with black along the edge and about 2cm across. The Saint John referred to in the name is John the Baptist; the plant played an integral part in celebrations of the Saint's day (24th June).

COMMON MILKWORT *Polygala vulgaris*
Milkwort flowers shine like sapphires among summer pastures but the colour is variable — usually blue, sometimes pink, even white. The individual flowers are unusually shaped with three small outer sepals, two large deeply coloured sepals and three small inner petals fused into a whitish fringed tube. These are produced on an inflorescence woven or trailing among other herbs or grasses. The stem is between 10 and 30cm long, woody at the base, with lance-shaped leaves up to 35cm long, the biggest nearest to the tip.

This is one of the favourite flowers of those country people who spend much of their time out of doors and have the opportunity to appreciate beauty in miniature.

COMMON ROCKROSE
Helianthemum nummularium
At its best on chalk downland or on the sunny slopes of limestone dales, this is usually a lime-loving plant found in open grassland or among light scrub. It is a perennial growing from a creeping rootstock or tap root and woody stem to a height of 5—30cm. The leaves are narrow, paired or opposite, and persist for most of the year. The plant is in flower for a long time too (from June to September), the striped buds opening

to produce a series of attractive flowers with large paper-thin, sulphur-yellow petals.

Various *Helianthemums* are cultivated in rock gardens but, as is so often the case, none has the simple grace of the wild variety.

MAIDEN PINK *Dianthus deltoides*
This is one of the least common flowers to be mentioned in this book but it represents a large and distinguished family. Pinks or wild carnations are one of the finest sights of Alpine and Pyrenean meadows, and also struggle to survive in this country. The maiden pink is the only species to be widespread, found locally on dry undisturbed pastures or sandy slopes at low altitude throughout Britain.

A perennial with a creeping stem, maiden pink grows in tufts or clumps to a height of 20 or 30cm. The leaves are narrow, grey-green in colour with fringes of fine hairs along the edges and underneath the main vein. The flowers are out from June to September. They are usually solitary and measure about 18mm across. Maiden pink has no scent, unlike several closely related species, but it is still pollinated by insects, especially moths which have long tongues and can reach down the calyx tube. The five rose-coloured petals have a tooth edge or fringe. At their base there is a darker line marking a delicate ring around the opening of the calyx, and outside this there is a dusting of pale freckles.

COMMON MOUSE-EAR
Cerastium fontanum
Mouse-ears are members of the same family as pinks and campions but have small white flowers and are often overlooked. The name came into common usage when mice were far more plentiful around kitchen gardens. The hairy-leaved weeds must have reminded cottagers of their unwelcome guests.

Common mouse-ear grows in waste ground and gardens as well as lawns and meadows, and is in flower from April until the first autumn frosts. It is a perennial, with trailing stems and a flowering shoot growing to a height of 15 or 20cm. The leaves are opposite, growing rather sparsely on the stem, and are very hairy — the shape of rabbit rather than mouse ears. The flowers grow from branched stalks (also hairy) and measure up to 10mm across, usually less. Five green sepals, visible between the thin notched petals, and a group of ten stamens give the flower a starry quality.

A larger relative of mouse-ear is the garden plant **snow-in-summer**, which often grows wild along walls and banks close to cottage gardens.

MEADOW CRANE'S-BILL

Geranium pratense

These days this graceful herb is most commonly seen along uncut road verges but in the quiet corners of old pastures it sometimes grows in profusion. It is a perennial, growing to a height of between 40 and 80cm. The upper stem and flower stalks are covered with slightly sticky hairs, and the

leaves have a surface of flattened hairs making them furry to the touch. They are broad, up to 15cm across, but are deeply lobed and acutely toothed.

The flowers usually grow in pairs. They are large, 3 or 4cm across, saucer shaped with five petals, and of a lovely translucent blue/violet colour. Meadow crane's-bill flowers from June to September, after which the beak-like seed heads develop.

WHITE CLOVER *Trifolium repens*

Clovers are typical members of the trefoil family. They have been sown, or at least encouraged, in hay meadows and pastures for a thousand years and are able to 'fix' nitrogen and thereby improve the quality of the grass.

The ability to root from nodes along its creeping stem allows the perennial white or Dutch clover to colonise lawns and survive

An individual white clover and, below, a field of flowers

regular mowing. Hence it is a familiar sight, in leaf or in flower, from June to September. It usually grows to a height of 10—20cm. The leaves are typical of trefoils, made up of three evenly shaped leaflets often slightly notched at their tip, growing on a long thin stalk. There is usually a pale V-shaped line towards the base of each leaflet. The flowers are contained in a dense round or cone-shaped head growing on the top of a stalk sent up from a leaf axil. The flowers are 8 or 9mm long, white or sometimes pink, and are visited by bees.

RED CLOVER *Trifolium pratense*

This is a another abundant clover (see white clover, page 37), flowering from May to September, but this time growing to a height of 10—40cm and found in open meadows and pastures rather than lawns. The leaves have rather long leaflets, up to 30mm, and are a grey/green colour. They also have a pale 'V' in the middle of the leaf which is not so regularly shaped as in white clover and is sometimes small or absent. The flowers are deep pink/purple, in a dense cone-shaped head about 2 or 3cm across.

'Four-leaved clovers', lucky leaves with an extra leaflet, are most frequently found on red clover. The leaflets are counted as follows: 'one for fame, one for wealth, one for love and one for health'.

REST HARROW *Ononis reclinata*

Years ago this innocuous but tough-stemmed herb had a reputation for stopping a harrow in its tracks. Rest harrow is a characteristic plant of lime-rich grassland and sand dunes where it is a larval foodplant of the common blue butterfly.

This herb is a perennial member of the pea family with large pink flowers (out from June to September), up to 15mm long, similar in shape to broom or gorse. It is a spreading, trailing plant growing either in clumps or low across the surface of the ground. The leaves are serrated, up to 2cm long, and like the stem and leaf stalks are covered with fine sticky hairs.

HORSESHOE VETCH *Hippocrepis comosa*

This is a yellow-flowered vetch (along with kidney vetch and bird's-foot trefoil — see following entries) but quite distinctive in that the 6—8 flowers radiate in a single tier, evenly spread out, at the top of a long stem. The flowers are small, about 8mm, superficially resembling bird's-foot trefoil but smaller and

thinner. The pod succeeding the flower is disproportionately long, about 30mm, and is crinkly, splitting into segments shaped like horseshoes.

The main flowering season is May to July; by late August the plant seems to have vanished, the leaves being composed of little leaflets each no longer than 8mm. It is difficult to see among grasses and rarely grows more than 15—20mm high.

Horseshoe vetch is characteristic of dry chalk and limestone grassland and is local but prolific where it occurs. It thrives in sheep- or rabbit-cropped downland turf and disappears when regular grazing stops.

KIDNEY VETCH *Anthyllis vulneraria*
This distinctive member of the pea family
likes grassland on thin dry soils. It is
especially a coastal plant, but is sometimes
found on inland limestone or chalk pastures.
Kidney vetch is perennial, growing from a
woody rootstock, sometimes sending
straggling shoots among the surrounding
grass but then sending out an erect stem to a
height of 20—30cm.

The flower heads are produced from
mid- to late summer and usually grow in
pairs; each one is sphere shaped, like a
pompom of white wool with tiny yellow or
red flowers around the surface. The whole
head measures 3 or 4cm; the individual
flowers, made up of a densely hairy calyx and
yellow petals, measure 12—15mm in length.
After pollination (by bees) the calyx swells
and the petals wither and turn orange/brown.
The leaflets are blue/green, a series of 3 or 4
opposite pairs of narrow leaflets topped by a
much larger terminal leaflet.

BIRD'S-FOOT TREFOIL *Lotus corniculatus*
'Bacon-and-eggs' is still a universal name for
this little plant. It is one of those traditional
species that everyone seems to know. 'Trefoil'
is a misleading name as its leaf actually has
five leaflets each 15—20mm long, though the
lower pair are at the base of the stalk and are
more properly called stipules. The flowers are
up to 15mm long, typically pea shaped having
a small toothed calyx and petals forming keels
and wings. These are bright yellow in colour,
but the buds are often red; the combination of
the little curved red buds and the rounded
yellow petals has earned the plant its
colloquial name, but over 70 other less
appropriate country names have been
recorded, including old woman's toe-nails
and rosy morn.

Bird's-foot trefoil is a creeping perennial
growing 10—40cm long, flowering from June
to September.

Bird's-foot trefoil

SILVERWEED *Potentilla anserina*
Many wild plants were harvested in times of
famine and the porridge made from the roots
and stolons of silverweed probably saved the
life of many a crofter's child. Today we know
it as a low, creeping weed of car parks and
road verges though it is also found in
pastures and dune slacks.

It is a member of the cinquefoil family,
with luminous bright-yellow flowers, five
petalled and large — over 15mm across. The
flower stalks grow from the leaf axils. The
leaves usually grow in a rosette and are
pinnate with up to 12 pairs of main leaflets,
heavily toothed, alternating with much
smaller ones. Each lacy leaf is covered top
and bottom with silky hairs, making it shine
like silver. The flowers are usually out
between the months of June and August.

Individual flowers comprise four
greenish or purple-tinged sepals, without any
petals. The upper ones are female and bear
purple stigmas, the lower ones are male and
have stamens. The whole plant only grows to
a height of 20 or 30cm, which is one reason
for its ability to compete successfully in close-
cropped downland turf. It is in flower from
May to August.

SALAD BURNET *Sanguisorba minor*
The fresh-tasting but tiny leaves of this little
plant hardly seem worth the effort of finding
and picking, but it was once normal country
fare, probably consumed as a garnish rather
than as a main vegetable.

Salad Burnet is most abundant on chalk
and limestone grassland and is a perennial,
growing from a woody rootstock. The main
leaves are produced in a rosette and are
pinnate with 4 or 5 pairs of round, deeply
toothed leaflets. When crushed they give off a
smell of cucumber. The stem is branched and
is topped by a tightly packed globe-shaped
head of flowers which measures
approximately 10mm across.

*Salad Burnet's
globe-shaped
flower head
(above), and
the complete
plant*

LADY'S MANTLE

Alchemilla vulgaris agg.

The saucer-shaped leaves of lady's mantle are well known to hill walkers, but it is very difficult to put a precise name to the various different kinds that occur. Common lady's mantle is actually an aggregate of microspecies, their features varying. The plant is a perennial, growing from a thick rootstock to a height of 10—40cm. The flowers are tiny, comprising four yellow sepals and no petals, gathered in an inflorescence or flower head and appearing from mid- to late summer.

The leaves attract most attention, especially those at the base of the stem. Their size and shape (up to 15cm across, with 5—7 broad lobes, toothed and neatly pleated) are very distinctive. They are covered with fine hairs, and dew or rain (or water exuded from the plant itself during humid weather) tends to gather in them into mercury- or pearl-like pools. These distinctive drops of water which appear on the leaves when no rain has fallen were once considered magical and were collected for use in alchemy. At the same time the plant had a reputation as a cure-all for women's ailments, especially sagging breasts, and the dew was once sold as a cosmetic.

AGRIMONY *Agrimonia eupatoria*

The tall, stiff flower spike of agrimony is a common sight from June to September along dry roadside verges, especially in the south of England. The flowers are yellow, five petalled and rose shaped but only 5—8mm in

Agrimony with, left, detail of stem and flowers

diameter. They only open for three days, and if not pollinated by insects in this time the anthers bend towards the stigma and self-pollination occurs. The fruits or achenes are carried in 'sticky buds' or burrs. The stem grows from 30—60cm in height and is sometimes pink or red in colour, as are the leaf stalks and the hooks of the burrs. The leaves grow low down on the stem and are shaped like those of silverweed (page 40), pinnate, toothed and with miniature leaflets between the main ones.

A yellow dye used to be extracted from the agrimony plant, though this was a poor substitute for weld (a better source of dye — see mignonette, page 104). It was also a medicinal herb, especially useful as a gargle.

COW PARSLEY *Anthriscus sylvestris*
Banks of cow parsley brighten many a dull
verge in May and early June when other
umbellifer plants are only just in leaf. Cow
parsley or Queen Anne's lace produces
swathes of fern-like leaves, deeply sculpted
into an intricate skeleton of leaflets. The
stems are hollow and are up to a metre tall.
They carry 'umbels' or umbrella-shaped
platforms of small white flowers, which act as
eye-catching landing pads for flies and wasps,
thus encouraging pollination by insects which
might not otherwise be able to locate or land
on isolated flowers.

Another roadside umbellifer, flowering
at about the same time of the year but
commoner in the north of Britain than the
south, is **sweet Cicely**, *Myrrhis odorata*. This
has heavier, less finely sculpted foliage and
gives off a powerful smell of aniseed.

Common hogweed, *Heracleum sphondylium*,
often grows in similar situations to cow
parsley, but flowers a little later, has deeply
lobed rather than lacy leaves and is a more
robust plant.

PIGNUT *Conopodium majus*
Another umbellifer, pignut is similar to cow
parsley in having an umbrella-shaped flower
head of small (1—3mm) white flowers, but is
a much more delicate plant only growing to a
height of 30—50cm. The radical leaves,
appearing from the base of the plant, quickly
shrivel and are rarely noticed.

Pignut flowers from May to July and
grows abundantly in old pastures and
meadows where the soil is slightly acidic. It is
a perennial, growing from a fleshy tuber. Pigs
grazed on pastures were attracted by the
tuber's nutty taste, as were Victorian children.

COMMON SORREL *Rumex acetosa*
The word 'sorrel' means sour. It was, and still
is, used in sauces where its sharp flavour
complements fish dishes. Common sorrel is a
slender kind of dock and its general structure
is similiar to its more robust relatives. It
usually grows to a height of 30—50cm. The
leaves are quite different to common dock
(page 108), being arrow or lance shaped and

Common sorrel

rarely growing more than 10cm long. Those
growing from the base have long stalks, those
higher up the stem are virtually stalkless and
clasp the stem. All the leaves are shiny and
deep green, changing to a deep red in the
autumn. The flower stalks grow from the
upper leaf axils.

Sorrel is wind pollinated and the
flowers are small and green, tinged with red,
like most other docks. They are carried in
loose whorls, the male on one plant and the
female on another. This is an abundant plant
of old meadows, flowering in May and June
before the hay harvest, but it is also found
along roadsides and in woodland clearings.

GERMANDER SPEEDWELL
Veronica chamaedrys

Speedwells, of various shades of blue, are among the most cheerful of path-side flowers to 'speed you well' on your journey. Germander speedwell is one of the larger species, growing up to 20cm tall and competing with other grassland herbs to add a unique gentian-blue to a community of predominantly yellow, pink or white flowers.

Despite its delicate appearance it is a perennial and is able to root from the nodes (leaf joints) and thereby creep among grass stems before issuing a flowering stem. The leaves are bluntly triangular, short stalked

and hairy. The main stems have a distinctive fringe of silky hairs on either side, but the flower spikes, which grow from the axils of the upper leaves, usually have a more general covering of fine hairs. The flowers, which are out from March to July, grow in a loose raceme or spike and measure about 1cm across. The blue corolla has four petal lobes with, at its centre, a white ring surrounding a shady 'pupil' — the origin of the plant's alternative name, bird's eye.

Germander speedwell lasts only a few minutes if picked. Even if you sit and try to draw the flower *in situ* it is quite likely that the corolla will have fallen off before you have finished.

COMMON CENTAURY
Centaurium erythraea

Centaury is related to the gentians and like them it is notable for the vivid colour of its flowers, in this case pink rather than blue. A plant of dry grassland, either on chalk and limestone hillsides or on coastal dunes, centaury is an annual, starting as a rosette of broad leaves each about 5mm wide and up to 5cm long. From this rosette, a square, erect and rigid stem grows to a height of 10—30cm, bearing opposite pairs of leaves.

The unusual formality of the whole plant is softened by the much less rigid arrangement of the flowers, in a loose head or growing from side shoots rising acutely from leaf axils. The flowers, which are out from June until the autumn, are pink, five petalled, fused into a corolla tube and measure about 10mm across. This is a plant that always seems to grow in interesting places. Where there is centaury there are usually other good things to look out for too.

COWSLIP *Primula veris*

A close relative of the primrose (page 21), with which it sometimes hybridises, this is also among the most popular of spring flowers and a barometer to the changing face of the countryside.

The word cowslip is derived from 'cow-slop', for the plant was once thought to grow where cow-pats had been freshly deposited. In fact it is a perennial and grows from rhizomes, thus appearing in the same place

year after year. The leaves are similar to those of the primrose, 5—15cm long, oval but tapering towards the base, and with a very wrinkled surface. The stem is comparatively sturdy and downy, usually 10—20cm tall, headed by a cluster of drooping flowers. These are funnel shaped, the corolla five lobed, deep yellow or orange in colour, and heavily scented.

COMMON EYEBRIGHT
Euphrasia nemorosa

This tiny annual herb, semi-parasitic like yellow rattle (page 49), was once used as a treatment for eye disorders because the flowers resembled diseased eyes, with 'purple and yellow spots and stripes'. Common eyebright is abundant in meadows and heathland from July until September, but because it is so small — between 10 and 20cm in height — it is easily overlooked. The leaves are oval, deeply toothed and often purple tinged. The flowers have a two-lipped corolla,

up to 8mm long, whitish with purple stripes and a yellow central smudge. The upper lip of the corolla is small with two main lobes, the lower of which is bigger and has three main lobes. There are 24 other species of eyebright, all very similar.

WILD THYME *Thymus praecox*

Thymol, the oil that gives this plant its appetising smell, is mildly antiseptic. Thyme is a miniature shrub, a perennial with surprisingly tough stems, forming mats in favourable places on dry rocky outcrops on all kinds of grassland, dunes and heaths where the soil is not too acidic. It grows to a height of only 5 or 6cm. The flowering shoots, which grow from a long branching stem, are square in cross section, two sides hairy and two smooth. The leaves are oval and about 5mm long. The rich pink-purple flowers grow in a dense spike and are composed of an upper and lower lip. They can be seen from the months of May to August.

Wild thyme does not have such a pungent smell as **garden thyme**, which is of Mediterranean origin, or as **large thyme**, *Thymus pulegioides*, which grows in south-east England.

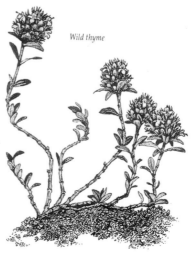

Wild thyme

Cow parsley

Top right: *Agrimony*
Middle right: *Pignut*
Bottom right: *Germander speedwell*
Below: *Wild thyme*

Selfheal

Ox eye daisy

Common eyebright

Cross-leaved heath

Yellow rattle

Early purple orchid

Mountain everlasting

Top right: *Mountain pansy*
Middle right: *Marsh violet*
Bottom right: *Heath milkwort*

Common spotted orchid

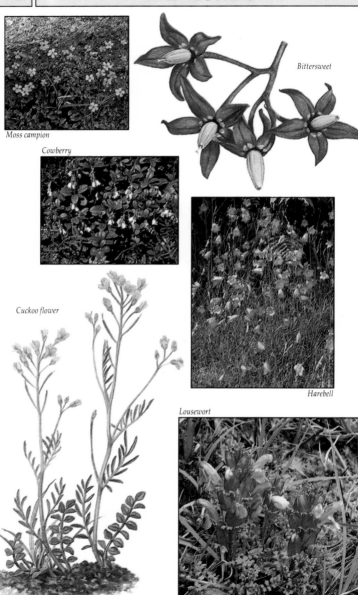

Moss campion

Bittersweet

Cowberry

Cuckoo flower

Harebell

Lousewort

SELFHEAL *Prunella vulgaris*

This is a plant of supposed medicinal properties in times past, and an attractive herb of road verges, old lawns and pastures. It is in flower from June to September. Selfheal is a perennial, growing from creeping runners to a height of up to 20cm. The leaves are opposite, smooth and oval, tapering towards the tip. The flowers are produced in a solid, square-shaped or oblong head made up of purple/brown bracts and calices and paler,

deep-violet corollas. Similar to that of the dead-nettle in shape, the corolla is 10—14mm long and has a large hooded upper lip and a split lower lip. The plant is pollinated by bees which are able to force their way between the corolla lips and reach down to the nectar.

YELLOW RATTLE *Rhinanthus minor*

Otherwise known as hay or corn rattle, this is an ever-present element of old hay fields and is a welcome sight to naturalists. It is a semi-parasite, stealing at least some of its food from grass roots, and not helping the hay crop. To farmers a hayfield colourful with yellow rattle is a sign of bad husbandry.

Yellow rattle is an annual, usually 20—30cm tall and flowering from May to July. It has opposite lance-shaped leaves, toothed and stemless, and the leafy flower spike is dominated by a bunch of inflated air-filled calices. These start out pale straw-green.

When the blunt, laterally compressed corollas have fallen, however, the calices turn brown and harden, and the seeds inside rattle if the stem is shaken.

RIBWORT PLANTAIN *Plantago lanceolata*

Most people know ribwort plantain by sight, which is unusual for a wind-pollinated plant. The leaves grow in a rosette and are long, narrow and strongly ribbed with three, sometimes five, parallel veins. They grow from a rootstock and the whole plant is able to persist from year to year despite cropping or cutting — thus it is commonly encountered in all but the most carefully manicured lawns.

The flower head is tall (30cm or more) with a deeply furrowed, tough and stringy stalk and a short solid inflorescence. The flowers that make up the head have green calices and brown corollas, typical colours for species that do not need to attract insects. A ruff or halo of white dancing anthers adds a touch of delicacy to this plant. It flowers from April to August.

Ribwort plantain

CROSSWORT *Galium cruciata*

Crosswort is found on most kinds of grassland if the soil is not acidic. It is a member of the bedstraw family (see next entry, lady's bedstraw, for comparison) but differs from bedstraws in being covered by downy hair. The stem is tall, up to 50cm, and the leaves grow in whorls or tiers all the way up — those in the middle are usually the longest at about 2.5cm. Each whorl is made up of a cross comprising four oval or egg-shaped leaves, each three-veined. These are broader than the leaves of other bedstraws.

The honey-scented flowers are very small, simple four-lobed corollas, yellow in colour, growing in clusters from the leaf axils. They can be found in May and June. In open situations such as road verges, crosswort

Crosswort (left) and lady's bedstraw (right)

LADY'S BEDSTRAW *Galium verum*

Bracken was once cut as bedding for cattle, but farmers and country folk collected bedstraw for their own mattresses. Not only was it free, comfortable and hay scented, it also deterred fleas and lice and was very easily renewed.

Lady's bedstraw (named after 'Our Lady', the Virgin Mary, who, in legend at least, gave birth on a bed of *Galium verum*) is a creeping perennial with straggling stems. These grow to a height of 20—50cm, and are square in section and slightly rough to the touch. Along the stems are whorls of 8—12 thin leaves, each with a single vein. The flowers are 2 or 3mm across and bright yellow, with four pointed petal-like lobes, appearing in dense terminal clusters. Lady's bedstraw adds a distinctive splash of gold to dry hedge banks, heaths and pastures during July and August.

grows in obvious clumps, the whorls remaining close together, but in deep grass the stem elongates and the plant sprawls among surrounding vegetation. Its yellow/green foliage makes it an easy plant to spot at a distance.

FIELD SCABIOUS *Knautia arvensis*

Dry grassy banks and downs are the traditional places for scabious. There are three species, the **devil's bit, small** and **field scabious**; all are hairy, the latter especially so. The name comes from scabies, an itchy skin disorder which the plant was reputed to cure.

Field scabious is a perennial, with a rosette of simple lance-shaped, slightly lobed leaves growing from a rootstock. The flower stem, which can grow to a height of a metre if the surrounding vegetation is dense, carries more variable leaves, often deeply fingered. By contrast devil's bit has lance-shaped leaves on the stem. The flower head of the field scabious comprises up to 50 florets, these being four lobed and lilac/blue in colour. The inner florets are small and pink tinged, whilst

Yarrow

Flower head of field scabious

the outer ones are more inclined to blue and have the marginal lobes enlarged. This is a flower which can be seen in high summer (late June to early September).

YARROW *Achillea millefolium*

All but the poorest, wettest grassland will support yarrow. It is widely known as milfoil or thousand-leaf, because of the feathery nature of its foliage, and is a member of the *Compositae* — the same large family that contains dandelions and daisies. It is almost as widespread, appearing in June and continuing in flower into the autumn. Yarrow grows from stolons to a height of 20—40cm, sending out downy shoots and the characteristic lacy, heavily dissected leaves.

The flower heads are about 5mm across, a little like the daisy in structure with a core of cream-coloured disc florets surrounded by a border of ray florets. These are white or pale pink, and there are usually five to a head. The heads are grouped into a dense, level-topped or umbrella-shaped platform.

Yarrow was a popular wound herb and is still used as such in some European countries. It has such an antiseptic smell that is not hard to imagine a medicinal value for what might otherwise be dismissed as a wayside weed.

OX EYE DAISY *Leucanthemum vulgare*
Motorway verges and grassy banks often
have an eye-catching display of these giant
daisies from June to August. It is a flower that
everyone knows by a different name; moon
daisy and marguerite are attractive
alternatives. Botanists sometimes still call it
by its old name *Chrysanthemum leucanthemum*.

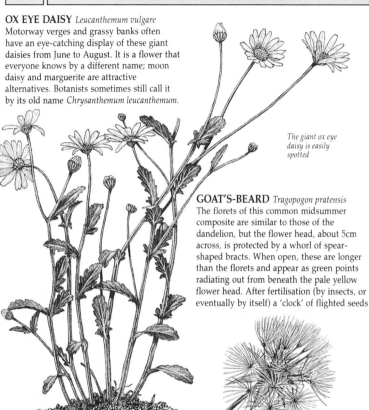

*The giant ox eye
daisy is easily
spotted*

GOAT'S-BEARD *Tragopogon pratensis*
The florets of this common midsummer
composite are similar to those of the
dandelion, but the flower head, about 5cm
across, is protected by a whorl of spear-
shaped bracts. When open, these are longer
than the florets and appear as green points
radiating out from beneath the pale yellow
flower head. After fertilisation (by insects, or
eventually by itself) a 'clock' of flighted seeds

It grows most abundantly on land of better
quality, such as meadows and cornfields.

The basal leaves and lower stem leaves
are rounded or spoon shaped with broad
lobes and long stalks. Those high on the stem
are thinner, more obviously toothed and
without stalks. The stems branch into tall
flower stalks, the plant reaching a height of
30—60cm. The flower heads are large, 3—5cm
across, and have yellow disc florets
surrounded by a border of 20 or more long
white ray florets.

is produced, like those of the dandelion but
bigger and more robust with fewer seeds in
each clock. Goat's-beard is an annual or a
biennial, growing from a tap root. It is usually
30—40cm tall, the long narrow leaves growing
from the base and lower stem.

Jack-go-to-bed-at-noon is another name
for this plant. It opens soon after dawn and
closes around midday — hence it is most
often recognised in its closed state, with its
bracts tightly shut over the florets. A closely
related species, **salsify**, has an edible root,
sometimes available from greengrocers.

KNAPWEED *Centaurea nigra*

Common or black knapweed is a plant of downs and traditionally managed meadows and pastures, and is especially attractive to butterflies in the prime time of July and August. It is a perennial, closely related to thistles but without the prickles, and varies in height 20—60cm depending on the state of the surrounding herbage. The lower leaves

are stalked, lance shaped and slightly toothed. Those further up the stem may be lobed, whilst those at the top are simple and stalkless. The lower bracts or involucre beneath the florets on the flower head form a solid, almost woody, mass and have a covering of dark-brown, triangular, overlapping scales fringed by paler bristles. This 'hard head' (yet another name for the plant) is topped by a bright red/purple tuft of florets, the whole flower head measuring 3—4cm across.

A closely related species, **greater knapweed**, is found in similar habitats, mostly in the south. It is larger and its flower head has an outer circle of longer florets, giving it an attractive halo.

HAWKWEED *Hieracium*

The above name actually covers about 250 closely related species in this country alone. Although often seen, individual hawkweeds are extremely difficult to identify and it is a good idea to enjoy them without trying to apply labels.

Hawkweeds are perennials, superficially like branched dandelions (page 116), but the florets in the flower head are not backed by long green bracts and the leaves grow up the stem. One of the commonest species is *H. vulgatum*, a roadside plant which flowers in June and July. Many hawkweeds are found in upland habitats and the greatest array can be seen from the Pennines northwards.

One of the many varieties of hawkweed, mouse-ear hawkweed H. pilosella

EARLY PURPLE ORCHID *Orchis mascula*
Orchids have always had a special mystique but many of the British species are disappointingly dull or obscure. Not so the early purple which is sturdy and colourful. Like most of our *Orchis* species it is a perennial, overwintering as a pair of egg-shaped tubers. From these grow a rosette of lance-shaped leaves, 10—15cm long, parallel veined and usually heavily marked with dark-purple blotches.

A pair of early purple orchids

The flower spike grows from the heart of the rosette, a spiral of leaves rising with the stem. The full-grown spike is 25cm or more in height and is topped by a loose raceme or head of flowers. These are bright red/purple and of typical orchid structure, three petals alternating with three sepals in a complex arrangement producing a hood and a lip. Two of the sepals point outward whilst the rear one and two of the petals form the hood. The remaining petal, much broader, forms a wide three-lobed lip which is spotted with purple.

The early purple orchid grows in several very different habitats, particularly in base-rich grassland and in woodland clearings. It lives up to its name by being early to flower, in April and May.

COMMON SPOTTED ORCHID
Dactylorhiza fuchsii
In most places this is the commonest of the summer orchids (it flowers from June to August). Similar in general structure to the previous species though not closely related, it has a much denser head of flowers which starts out conical but soon turns cylindrical as the spike reaches maturity. The flowers are pink or sometimes white, the lower lip broad and three lobed, the central lobe longer than the others, dotted and streaked with purple. The leaves growing up the stem are keeled and lance shaped, but the lowest leaves of the rosette are almost oval. They are usually marked with transverse oblong blotches (those in the early purple run down rather than across the leaves). Sometimes, especially in the white-flowered form, the upper surfaces of the leaves are plain dark green.

In ideal conditions, on damp grassy banks and meadows with neutral or basic soils, spotted orchids can produce extensive colonies and the individual plants sometimes develop flower heads over 10cm tall.

HEATH, MOOR AND MOUNTAIN

*H*igh hills and northern moors can be grey and forbidding places. Rainfall and impeded drainage keep the ground waterlogged, prevent the formation of humus and wash minerals out of the soil. The result is a surface of peat, of high acidity and low fertility. The sandy heaths of southern England have many features in common with moorlands. Bright green patches on a heath or moor indicate where bogs or mires have formed. Standing water is capped by a spongy layer of Sphagnum or bog moss with an interesting tracery of flowers growing over the surface.

Drier moorland is usually colonised by heather. The traditional management of grouse moors on the large estates of northern England and Scotland is based on the burning of the old heather to encourage fresh shoots, resulting in a patchwork of dense, knee-deep vegetation.

Driving along moorland roads is so exhilarating that it is easy to think of the wide rolling uplands as Britain's final wilderness. In fact, overgrazing has changed the vegetation of these windswept places, encouraging coarse grasses at the expense of heather. Grouse shooting is a costly business and is not particularly widespread these days, so the moors are less well managed. Drainage, in the form of parallel trenches or 'sheep grips', scars the Pennines from the Peak District to the Cheviots, and even the sodden layer of blanket bog which may have dominated the high ground since Neolithic times is being pushed back to allow farming to extend higher into the hills.

Considerable areas of our finest landscape, even in such classic hill country as the Lake District, are very dull when seen in detail. Walkers are used to the constant presence of just a few flowers such as heath bedstraw and tormentil, but it is worth searching out less popular sites where a much greater variety of plants can be found.

True mountain flowers are often restricted in this country to the very highest and most rugged ground, to the Cairngorms and Snowdonia and other remote rocky outcrops above 700m, though many good sites are only a short walk from roads. In the extreme north and west of Scotland it is even possible to find alpines growing at sea level.

ALPINE LADY'S MANTLE
Alchemilla alpina

Most people never see alpine plants because they never get high enough, but this cut-leaved relative of the common lady's mantle descends almost to sea level on crags, screes and pastures in both the north of England and Scotland.

Alpine lady's mantle is a perennial growing from a tough rootstock to a height of 10 or 15cm. The leaves are about 3cm across and made up of five separate fingers, toothed towards the tips. The uppersides are dark green, contrasting with the undersides which are shiny silver and covered with down. The flowers grow in dense terminal clusters but are very small, no more than 3mm across, with four green sepals and no petals. The plant is in flower from June to September.

MOUNTAIN PANSY *Viola lutea*

This is one of the most beautiful of our violets. It is found on lime-rich soils where any calcium has been washed or leached away, on basalt ridges, and beside streams leading from lead mines where heavy metals have been deposited.

Mountain pansy is a creeping perennial, flowering from May to August. The lower leaves are spoon shaped and lobed, those further up the stem are thin and more lance shaped. The flower differs from the closely related heartsease (page 104) in its larger size, up to 3cm across, and the greater length of its lower lip and spur. The colour forms of mountain pansy are all yellow, deep purple or a combination of the two.

MARSH VIOLET *Viola palustris*

An unusual violet in its choice of habitat, this species is most often found among saturated bog moss alongside moorland burns and becks. It is a perennial, producing a long creeping rhizome from which grow loose tufts of leaves. The leaves are long stalked, broader than the heart-shaped leaves of other violets

and up to 4cm across, looking almost round or kidney shaped. They are a similar dark green, with dimpled or bluntly toothed edges.

It is as well that the leaves are so distinctive because the flowers, which are a subdued lilac or off-white with purple veins, are often absent even during the main season of April to July.

MOSS CAMPION *Silene acaulis*
Most real mountain flowers are compact and brightly coloured, and this campion is an excellent example. It forms dense diminutive cushions of mossy foliage with simple lance-shaped leaves; the whole plant grows to about 10cm tall, the individual leaves about 1cm long. By comparison, the flowers are large, about 1cm across, bright rose-red in colour and five petalled.
They are similar in

structure to other campions (see red campion, page 14 and sea campion, page 94) and the male and female flowers are carried on separate plants.

Moss campion flowers in July and August and is found on spectacular mountains in the west and north, from Snowdonia to the Scottish Islands. It also grows at sea level in the extreme north.

HEATH MILKWORT *Polygala serpyllifolia*
Milkwort seems to grow everywhere, but in fact there are several species specialising in different habitats. One is found on southern chalk hills, another is widespread on acid moors and heaths where chalk and lime are entirely absent. Heath milkwort is very similar in appearance to common milkwort (page 35); both are creeping perennials with small lance-shaped leaves and attractive

flowers. These are composed of three small outer sepals, two laterally compressed larger sepals and a fused inner tube made up of three petals. Heath milkwort usually has more slate-coloured flowers, less intensely blue than its relatives, and its lower leaves are opposite rather than alternate. It flowers from June through to September.

TRAILING ST JOHN'S WORT
Hypericum humifusum
This little plant lives up to its name by being a trailing or sprawling member of a family that includes some tall and stately species. It is very dainty, rarely growing more than 20cm long, with a slender stem and fine oval leaves. These are opposite, and are dotted with tiny glands, like pinholes.

The flowers are comparatively small (about a centimetre across) and sparse compared with the packed heads of some of the taller species, such as perforate St John's wort (page 35). The five rather narrow petals are orange/yellow, and are a little longer than the green sepals that they cover. Trailing St John's wort is a plant of dry acid soils and is most common on the heaths of the south and west. It flowers from June to September.

Trailing St John's wort

GORSE *Ulex europaeus*

The yellow pigment in gorse (isoliquiritigenum) can be used as a treatment for heartburn. Unfortunately gorse also contains quantities of the same poison that is found in laburnum, so eating the flowers might do more harm than good!

Gorse is usually a plant of dry acid soils, on the edges of heaths and moors. It often grows on ground once cultivated but now reverted to waste or heath, and is a

Thickets of gorse bring a splash of yellow to moorlands

useful clue to archaeologists looking for signs of prehistoric settlements. It is a dense, often impenetrable shrub, up to 2m tall, covered with long furrowed spines. The flowers, about 15mm long, can be found from Christmas to midsummer and are composed of a downy calyx and slightly longer corolla, bright yellow in colour. The scent is very heavy; to sit in the shade of a gorse bush on a warm spring afternoon amid the sound of bees and the coconut scent of the flowers is wonderfully relaxing.

When the flowers have fallen, black seed pods up to 1.5cm long develop, snapping open on dry summer evenings to disperse the seeds.

BROOM *Cytisus scoparius*

'He who brings broom into the house in May Sweeps the head of the house away'.
Broom, the *Planta genista*, lent its name to the Plantagenet Dynasty and has had both magical and medicinal uses through the centuries. Why it should have become so unlucky for male householders (the superstition does not apply to women) is a complete mystery.

Broom belongs to the *Leguminosae*, the family that also includes gorse and the garden pea. It is similar to gorse in having a flower comprising calyx and corolla, the latter bright yellow and split into five lobes or petals, but the calyx is only one-quarter the length of the corolla and the whole flower is larger, up to 20mm long. Broom is a tall shrub, growing as high as gorse (up to 2m). The foliage is composed of narrow trifoliate leaves rather than spines, and finches and buntings do not find it such a good nesting place. The flowering season is May and June. Like gorse, broom is often found on lime-free soil, preferring sandy heaths and waysides.

TORMENTIL *Potentilla erecta*
In many overgrazed and impoverished upland pastures this modest little flower, in association with heath bedstraw (page 69), is the only relief from bracken and mat-grass. It is a relative of the cinquefoils, a creeping perennial growing from a stout red rootstock to a height of 10—15cm. The leaves usually have three leaflets, but an added pair of stipules often confuse the issue and make them look like miniature horse chestnut leaves. They are stemless, toothed and covered underneath by silky hairs.

Tormentil flowers are about 10mm across and usually have four petals (cinquefoils have five). They are kidney shaped, notched, and the flowers are carried on a long stalk growing from the leaf axils. The plant is in flower from mid- to late summer and is widespread over heaths, moors and pastures on most soils except chalk. The name comes from the Latin *tormentina* meaning colic; the plant was used as a folk remedy.

ROUND-LEAVED SUNDEW *Drosera rotundifolia*
Miniature 'meadows' of sundew are a wonderful sight — a hazy red carpet best viewed from ground level. Unfortunately the 'meadow' is often no more than a veneer over saturated *Sphagnum* moss. Sundew grows in treacherous places. It is an unexpectedly tiny plant, a circlet of low, long-stemmed, round leaves, out all summer, each about 1cm across and grouped around a tapered rootstock. Each leaf is covered with long red hairs, on the end of which are glands which produce clear sticky drops of liquid. Midges and other small insects become trapped in the glue, then part-enfolded in the leaves, and are gradually digested by the plant to provide it with nitrates. Sundew flowers are very ephemeral. Short lived, they are about 5mm across, six petalled and white in colour. They appear from mid- to late summer, opening one after another on a tall curled stem.

The sticky 'dew' on the leaves, which does not evaporate even in the heat of the sun, was once thought to have special virtues, so much that, according to the 17th-century herbalist Gerard, 'cattle of the female kinde are stirred up to lust by eating even of a small quantitie'.

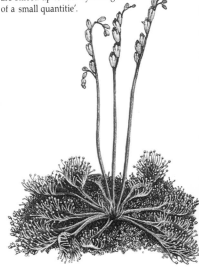

COWBERRY *Vaccinium vitis-idaea*

In much of northern Europe this is a plant of old pine woods, but in this country it is more likely to be encountered on open peaty moorland where it grows among heather and bilberry. It is a low evergreen shrub, the main flower-bearing stems rising from creeping

rhizomes to a height of 10—20cm. The leaves are similar in shape to those of the bilberry but are more leathery, turned down at the edges and dotted with glands underneath. The flowers are spherical or bell shaped, white tinged with pink, with a corolla about 6mm long.

Because it has comparatively large flowers which are out from June to August between the seasons of bilberry and heather, cowberry is easy to spot and is known by sight, if not by name, on acid hills and moors throughout Wales, the Pennines, and especially in Scotland. The berries are bright red and a little larger than those of bilberry. Although they are sometimes used by enthusiasts to make an ethnic Scottish form of cranberry jelly, they are virtually inedible.

CROWBERRY *Empetrum nigrum*

A creeping perennial shrub usually growing among heather on moors and mountains, crowberry has a superficial resemblance to a species of *Erica* or heath (see cross-leaved heath, page 62). The stems are red and covered with down or hair. The leaves are parallel sided, roll edged and about 5mm long. The flowers are unlike any of the heaths, however, being spiky and composed of six narrow pink sepals. They are only 1 or 2mm across and are wind pollinated, the male and female flowers being carried on different plants. Crowberry is out in May and June. In late summer the female plants carry small purple/black berries which are about 5mm across, tasteless, but still eaten by Laplanders.

Crowberry is a plant of the uplands but it has a few outposts in the east and south-west, on dry peaty heaths.

Crowberry

BILBERRY *Vaccinium myrtillus*

Bilberry is a low shrub of dry upland heaths
and moors growing to a height of up to 60cm,
though this depends very much on the degree
of sheep grazing. It is deciduous and during
the winter its blunt, four-sided stems look
stark and artificially bare. The foliage
develops in the early spring; the fresh green
leaves, 1—3cm long and slightly toothed,
contrast with the heather among which the
plant grows.

The flowers appear in April and May,
growing singly or in pairs from the leaf axils.
They can be mistaken for fruits at a distance,
being round and reddish. Closer examination
reveals a short calyx and an almost spherical
corolla about 5mm long. This is waxy, pink
with a greenish base and pale lipped rim, the
shape of an inverted urn. The real fruits
develop in July and August and are deep
purple or black with a bloom like untouched
grapes. They are about 8mm across.
Sometimes there are only a few on a bush,
perhaps because grouse and voles have
reaped the harvest first. However, if there are
enough they are well worth picking.

HEATHER *Calluna vulgaris*

One of the abiding memories of travellers to
the slopes of Kilimanjaro is seeing forests of
heather, the plants towering 7 or 8m tall. In
Britain, common heather (not of the same
genus) is usually 50 or 60cm tall, often much
less than that when it is managed to provide
food and cover for grouse. It still dominates
many upland landscapes, turning many hills
purple during August and September.

*Heather's small flowers can,
collectively, create a sea of purple*

Heather prefers well-drained lime-
deficient soils and thrives on moors and
heaths. It is a perennial, its stems woody and
branching, and has an evergreen covering of
very short leaves (1 or 2mm long). These are
triangular in cross section and in four rows
up the stem. The flowers are small, 4 or 5mm,
and are pale pink/purple, occasionally white,
in colour. They appear in a dense

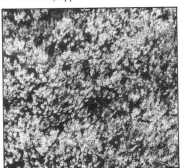

inflorescence and remain in a folded papery
state for months afterwards. The calyx is
longer than the corolla and covers it; what
appears to look like the calyx is in fact a
quartet of bracts.

Until the turn of the century heather, or
ling, was pervasive in the English uplands
and was used as a material for bedding, fuel
and thatching.

BELL HEATHER *Erica cinerea*
Bell heather is not a true heather but a
heath, similar in size and general appearance
to cross-leaved heath but with hairless leaves,
carrying the narrower, bright-purple flowers
in more profuse clusters. The leaves are in
whorls, this time
three together.

Bell heather is in flower from July to
September. It sometimes grows on its own
along road verges through sandy heaths but
more often it appears on the same moors as
cross-leaved heath, indicating where the
driest ground is to be found. People who
gained a living from the moors called this and
cross-leaved heath 'she heather' to
distinguish them from the more virile, less
elegant 'he-heather', meaning common heather.

CROSS-LEAVED HEATH *Erica tetralix*
Heaths differ from heathers in having the
calyx much shorter than the corolla. Cross-
leaved heath is a downy perennial, growing
on heather moors but always in the wetter

places where the peat is getting boggy. The
leaves are 3 or 4mm long, in obvious whorls
or tiers of four at a time. The flowers, with a
pink oval corolla 6 or 7mm long, grow in
dense, slightly drooping heads. Despite being
so different to common heather this is an
easy plant to miss. It grows only to about
30cm and forms restricted communities
around mires or along clogged drainage
channels. It flowers in July and August.

CRANBERRY *Vaccinium oxycoccos*
The delicate stems of cranberry usually form
an open tracery over hummocks of bog moss
on upland mires, like loose threads of cotton
over a quilt. The evergreen leaves, alternate
and widely spaced along a trailing stem, are
only 5 or 6mm long. They are oval and rolled
at the edges, dark shiny-green in colour,
sometimes turning red. The flowers are
composed of four deep-pink corolla lobes or
petals, about 5mm long, recurved back over a
short calyx almost to touch themselves,
leaving exposed a tube of yellowish stamens.
The flowers usually droop on the end of S-
shaped stalks, 1 or 2 together. They are out in
June and July and give way to red-mottled
berries, up to 8mm across, which can be seen
in September and October.

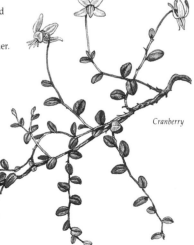

Cranberry

DODDER *Cuscuta epithymum*

Dodder is an odd name for a very odd plant, a parasite unable to support itself. It is without any chlorophyll or green pigment, and without any real leaves, these being reduced to tiny scales. It is an annual, sending a red thread-like stem twining and scrambling around heather or gorse bushes. It then sends suckers into their tissue and absorbs their food.

Its flowers are more conventional, appearing in July and August. They are small, about 3mm across, pink and with five corolla lobes or petals, and densely grouped in stalkless heads. Dodder is a local plant of southern heathland, but where it occurs it is quite common, transforming pathsides of heather from green to pink as it swathes them in clinging threads and posies of innocuous-looking flowers.

HEATH SPEEDWELL *Veronica officinalis*

Speedwells might appropriately be called travellers' flowers, familiar acquaintances of people on the move (see also germander speedwell, page 43). The heath speedwell, sometimes — and confusingly — called the common speedwell, is no exception and must have been a constant companion of drovers and shepherds when much of the country was heath or common land, criss-crossed by dusty pathways. It is a low-growing perennial herb, with long creeping stems and flower spikes growing from leaf axils to a height of about 10cm. The leaves are opposite, short stalked and about 2cm long. They are spear shaped, oval or broad, bluntly toothed and hairy both top and bottom.

The flower spike of heath speedwell is very attractive, pyramidal and compact, and is composed of lilac/blue flowers. They measure 5 or 6mm across and are of the usual speedwell structure with five lobes arising from a very short corolla tube, and two spiky stamens sticking out like mouse whiskers. The flowers are out from May to August, wherever there are dry grassy heaths and old track verges.

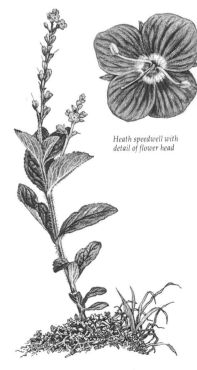

Heath speedwell with detail of flower head

LOUSEWORT *Pedicularis sylvatica*
The flowers of lousewort often seem
disproportionately large compared with the
rest of the plant. Lousewort is a multi-
stemmed perennial growing from a thick
rootstock. These stems trail over the ground
before sending up low flower spikes 5—10cm
high. The leaves grow around the base and up
the stem; they are up to 2cm long, dark green,
deeply toothed or dissected, each tooth
bearing several lobes. Up to 10 flowers are
carried on each raceme or head. They are
composed of a long, smooth, five-sided calyx
with four rather strange leafy lobes at the
mouth, and a dark-pink corolla. This is more
than 2cm long, separated into an upper lip
with two teeth and a lower lip with three
large lobes.

Lousewort is semi-parasitic, taking at
least some food from the roots of adjacent
moorland plants. It grows on impoverished
acid soils, on moors and damp heaths, and is
out between April and August. A closely
related species, **marsh lousewort**, *P. palustris*,
is an annual which grows on even boggier
ground, is taller and single stemmed, and has
a hairy calyx.

BUTTERWORT *Pinguicila vulgaris*
A very singular plant of mineral-rich flushes,
moorland burns, open peat and wet rocks,
butterwort was, like the buttercup,
traditionally hung up in cowsheds to keep
milk-curdling spirits at bay.

Common butterwort is a perennial
growing from an overwintering bud, from
which a rosette of pale yellow/green radical
leaves develops. These leaves are unusually
thick, 2—8cm long, curled at the sides and

have a greasy or sticky secretion on their
upper surfaces. Small flies become trapped,
whereupon the leaves curl inwards and
release chemicals which dissolve any parts of
the insects which are soft and digestible.
Nitrogen is probably the pay-off.

Butterwort has a short flowering
season, between May and July. Leafless
stalks, slightly S-shaped and up to 15cm high,
rise from the centre of the rosette, each
bearing a single flower. This has a violet
corolla over 10mm across, composed of a
broad two-lobed upper lip and a much larger
and even broader three-lobed lower lip, white
mouthed and with a narrow spur.

Marsh marigold

Gipsywort

Heath spotted orchid

Water crowfoot

Yellow water-lily

Sneezewort

Mare's tail

Ragged robin

Himalayan balsam

Great willow-herb

Frosted orache

Common hogweed

Stork's-bill

Bogbean

Purple loosestrife

Monkey flower

Sea milkwort

Valerian

Vipers bugloss

Northern marsh orchid

Sea campion

Yellow-horned poppy

HAREBELL *Campanula rotundifolia*
Harebell, sometimes called the Scottish
bluebell, is characteristic of dry grassy heaths,
dunes and well-drained pastures. Although its
flowers sometimes form clumps or patches
from July to September, it never carpets
spring woods or grassy western slopes the
way the bluebell (page 31) does.

Heath bedstraw

and grow to a height of about 20cm. The
stems and shoots are ridged and four sided,
hairless and with well-spaced whorls
comprising a collar of 6—8 leaves. Each leaf is
8—10cm long, broadest towards the tip, and
is edged by short bristly hairs. These make
the foliage rough to the touch. The flowers
are out from mid- to late summer, growing in
sparse clusters. They are very simple, about
3mm across, with a white, four-lobed corolla.

Harebell grows from stolons to a height
of 20—40cm. The leaves projecting from the
roots are about 1cm across, heart shaped and
toothed. Those growing from the stem
resemble short grass blades. The drooping
flowers are bell shaped, 15mm long, with five
pointed lobes to the corolla. They are very
papery and light, unlike those of the bluebell,
and are pale sky-blue in colour.

HEATH BEDSTRAW *Galium saxatile*
Scattered clouds of heath bedstraw flowers
relieve the monotony of many upland sheep
walks, often in company with tormentil and
harebell. The plant is almost universal on dry
acid heathland, pastures and verges. It forms
straggling carpets of branched stems, from
which flowering shoots rise. These are slender

MOUNTAIN EVERLASTING
Antennaria dioica
Many plants of windswept hilltops grow in
compact tussocks. Mountain everlasting is no
exception — it is a very short, very hairy
perennial with creeping stolons which send
up clumps or rosettes of spoon-shaped leaves
2 or 3cm tall. These are dark green above and
covered in white wool below. The flowers
grow in clusters on stems 5—20cm tall. The
male flowers are about 5mm across, with
white scaly bracts, like daisy florets, around
the outside. The female flowers are twice the
size, pink in colour.

Although mountain everlasting flowers
around midsummer, its dry woolly heads and
stems last much longer; once the seeds have
dispersed, they provide a passable alternative
to eidelweiss for British walkers who have
reached the high fells and are searching for a
memento of their journey.

AUTUMN HAWKBIT *Leontodon autumnalis*
Hawkbits are related to hawkweeds (page 53) and dandelions (page 116) but the flower stems are usually branched and the leaves grow from the base. Autumn hawkbit is a perennial with a rosette of narrow, dandelion-shaped leaves, heavily toothed and usually notched to the midrib. The stem grows to 30 or 40cm tall and is forked 2 or 3 times. The flower heads, about 3cm across, are composed

Autumn hawkbit (left) and bog asphodel (right)

BOG ASPHODEL *Narthecium ossifragum*
A member of the lily family with parallel-veined leaves, asphodel develops from a creeping rhizome into one of our most beautiful flowers. It is found, often in crowds, on most acid mires and raised bogs.

The spike grows to between 10 and 25cm tall and is topped by a head of yellow, star-shaped flowers. These are six petalled

and fragrant. After flowering in July and August the whole spike turns to rich saffron, then bleaches in the autumn frosts and persists through to the following year.

HEATH SPOTTED ORCHID
Dactylorhiza maculata
This is the common orchid of peaty soils. It resembles the common spotted orchid (page 54) but does not grow quite so tall or so luxuriantly. The leaves in its rosette are all lance or sword shaped and are heavily marked with round rather than the oblong blotches found on common spotted orchids.

The flower spike is usually conical, a mass of pale-pink or white flowers marked with purple. The lower lip of the flower is very prominent, the two outer lobes very broad and a little longer than the middle one. Heath spotted orchid is found on most kinds of heath and moor, wet and dry, and is in flower in July and August.

of yellow florets. The undersides of the outer florets are streaked with red, prominent in dull weather when the flowers close. Autumn hawkbit is a common plant of heathy grassland and is especially noticeable on roadside verges in the late summer and autumn. A closely related but much more hairy hawkbit, called **rough hawkbit,** *L. hispidus*, is found in more basic grassland.

RIVER, LAKE AND MARSH

*R*iverside footpaths provide some of the most pleasant of summer walks, mixing woodland and grassland with marsh and waterside habitats. In general, rivers in the south of England are likely to be slow flowing and clouded by sediment. Those in the north are likely to have a greater gradient so the current is faster, making them clear, cold and rich in oxygen. This has a considerable effect on the vegetation, which is more luxuriant and varied in the south, where flooding is less frequent and any silt deposited on the banks is full of nutrients.

Too much fertility can be very harmful to aquatic wildlife. If the nutrients flowing into a body of water are too great there is a risk that algae will have a population surge and form a bloom like pea soup which takes all the oxygen from the water and kills plants and animals. This problem is much worse than it used to be: fertilisers applied by farmers to their crops usually end up in rivers and lakes, spoiling the natural balance. Water full of nutrients is called 'eutrophic', and the process of enrichment is known as 'eutrophication'.

Lakes, ponds and old canals usually have rich communities of aquatic plants, either free-floating or rooted in the mud. They may also have margins of reeds and rushes forming a swamp zone, or newly colonised expanses of open mud. Lakes are always changing, always evolving. As soon as they are formed they begin to fill themselves in, and this is also the fate of artificially created reservoirs, ponds and canals.

Marshes and undrained fens, areas of nutrient-rich waterlogged soil or peat swamped by mineral-enriched water, are places of exceptional interest. Because the resulting soil is of such high quality most extensive fens have been drained and diminished, so only fragments of the original habitat are left. Wayside drains and ditches provide valuable alternatives to these magical places. They may not be beautiful but they do recreate ideal conditions for most of the flowers described in this section.

MARSH MARIGOLD *Caltha palustris*
'Molly blobs' is just one of many cheerful country names for this giant marshland buttercup. It flowers from March to May alongside streams, among fenland vegetation, and in wet woodland clearings and meadows. Sometimes it appears singly, at other times it crowds whole meadows.

Marsh marigold grows 20—40cm tall. The leaves rise from the base on long stalks and are broad and kidney shaped with finely toothed edges. They average 10cm across but after the plant has flowered they can grow much bigger. The flowers are 20—40mm across, with up to 100 stamens and five golden-yellow sepals (not petals).

LESSER SPEARWORT
Ranunculus flammula
Lesser spearwort is an unobtrusive marshland buttercup, flowering from early to late summer. It is a perennial with a rather thick hollow stem which spreads and roots over the waterlogged ground then rises abruptly to a height of 40 or 50cm. The leaves are spear shaped, sometimes slightly toothed or serrated, and those growing from the stem are thin and strap like. The flowers are between

Lesser spearwort

10 and 20mm across with five glossy-yellow petals, five greenish-yellow sepals and a core of short-stalked stamens.

Like Goldilocks (page 13), lesser spearwort only ever has a thin scattering of flowers and rarely dominates even where it is abundant. The scientific name *flammula* refers to the fiery and blistering effect which results from eating the foliage.

COMMON WATER CROWFOOT
Ranunculus aquatilis
In late May and June the surfaces of rich, slow-flowing streams and ponds are dusted with a confetti of white crowfoot flowers. There are a dozen closely related species of which *R. aquatilis* is the commonest. Crowfoots are aquatic buttercups. The flowers are similar in structure to those of land buttercups but are white with just a tinge of yellow at the bases of the petals. The rest of the plant is very different, adapted to life in water, rooted in sediment and with a submerged stem and leaves. These are so divided that they look more like clumps of threads or filaments waving in the current. Several species, including *R. aquatilis*, have additional floating leaves which are broad and lobed, quite unsuitable for aquatic life but ideal for making the most of sunlight striking the surface.

WHITE WATER-LILY *Nymphaea alba*

The massive floating flowers of white water-lily look suspiciously exotic but the plant is a true native, found throughout Britain in ponds and lakes with rich muddy sediments. It grows from a rootstock sending stems 2 or 3m to the surface. The floating leaves are plate shaped, 30cm across, and can bear the weight of moorhens. The flowers appear in July and August and are about 15cm across, floating by day but submerged at night. They have four outer sepals, yellowish-green on the outside and white inside, and up to 24 pure white, lance-shaped petals. The fruits ripen underwater and release seeds which float to the surface.

large rounded sepals, yellow but green tinged on the outsides, and a dense core of small yellow petals and stamens. The long stems send the flowers a few centimetres clear of the surface, making it look as if the water level has suddenly dropped. The fruit is flask shaped and the flowers have an alcoholic scent — which explains the flower's alternative name, brandy bottles.

White water-lily

YELLOW WATER-LILY *Nuphar lutea*

Chopped-up fragments of yellow water-lily leaves are a common sight among the flotsam of navigable waterways. The plant grows well in deep, slow-moving, well-shaded canals but rarely reaches maturity there. Elsewhere it thrives in dykes and ponds. Its floating leaves are distinguished from those of the white water-lily by being heart shaped and slightly pointed. The flowers are out in July and August. They are about 5cm across, with five

MARE'S-TAIL *Hippuris vulgaris*

Mare's-tail looks like a luxuriant kind of horsetail (a primitive non-flowering plant which gardeners know only too well). In fact it is a flowering plant, more closely related to water weeds such as water milfoil. Mare's-tail is an emergent plant, sending up broad stems from rhizomes buried in the muddy beds of calcium-rich lakes and slow-moving streams. The emergent part of the erect stem may be 30 or 40cm tall and resembles a bottle brush, with whorls of blunt leaves. Other submerged stems are more pliable with longer and less rigid leaves. The flowers, which are very insignificant, appear in June and July. They grow in leaf axils and are wind pollinated.

WINTER-CRESS *Barbarea vulgaris*
Allow a cabbage to run riot and it will produce a head of four-petalled flowers, the trade mark of the *Cruciferae*. Winter-cress is a typical crucifer of river banks and damp verges, and grows quite tall, to 40 or 60cm. The leaves are shiny, and those at the base are long and deeply lobed. The flowers are small, about 8mm across, yellow and four petalled. They grow in dense clusters at the

tips of stems and stalks sent up from leaf axils, and are out from spring to late summer. The stalks gradually elongate through the season to allow more flowers to develop above the thin, angular pods.

The foliage lasts well into the winter and was once used in salads when other greens were unobtainable.

CUCKOO FLOWER *Cardamine pratensis*
Damp meadows and verges are the typical habitat for this attractive spring flower, otherwise known as lady smock. Cuckoo flower is usually 20 or 30cm tall; it is a

perennial and sends up a rosette of long-stalked leaves divided into seven roundish leaflets, the end one much the largest. The leaflets of the stem leaves are thinner, almost thread like.

The flower head is on a tall stem which elongates as the plant runs to seed. Individual flowers are large, about 15mm across, four petalled and pale pink, sometimes almost white. Ripening seed pods often harbour well-camouflaged caterpillars of orange tip and green-veined white butterflies.

WATER-CRESS *Nasturtium officinale*
Strong in vitamin C, water-cress has been grown commercially for 200 years but it is common in the wild too, beside running water in lowland Britain. Unfortunately it attracts the liver-fluke, a parasite of beast and man, so the wild sort should not be eaten. Water-cress is a tall bushy plant, often 40 or 50cm high, with hollow stems and glossy green leaves divided into oval leaflets, the end one almost round. The flowers are white, four petalled and about 5mm across, growing in clusters at the head of the stem. The plant continues in flower from May to October, and the leaves can last right through the winter.

Water-cress

HIMALAYAN BALSAM

Impatiens glandulifera

As the name suggests this is an alien plant — it looks and smells exotic but is now at home along most river banks. It grows up to 2m high, its broad, hollow, red stems supporting a foliage of finely toothed lance-shaped leaves each about 10cm long. The deep-pink flowers,

3 or 4cm long, grow in an attractive spike and are slung beneath the stalks. They are distinctive in shape — five uneven petals grouped into a large upper and lower lip — with a deep hood behind which is a small curved spur.

Despite its size, Himalayan balsam is an annual, growing each year from seed and flowering from July to October. A closely related but smaller American species called **orange balsam** has also become naturalised on river banks and canal towpaths, whilst a third species, native to north-west Britain, is **touch-me-not**. The name describes the sudden explosive way in which all balsams catapult their seeds from the swollen cases.

RAGGED ROBIN *Lychnis flos-cuculi*

Drainage of marshes and wet meadows has seen a sad decline in ragged robin. It used to be known by every country child but in many places only the name lingers on, often applied in error to red campion (page 14). In fact the plants do have similarities — both are pink-flowered members of the campion family and are about 50cm tall. However, ragged robin is much more finely formed. The leaves are thin, those at the base broadening towards their tips. The flowers, measuring 3 or 4cm across, look tattered or frayed since each petal is deeply divided into four. It is a plant of fens, marshes and wet meadows, to be seen in late May and June.

MEADOWSWEET *Filipendula ulmaria*

The sickly-sweet smell of meadowsweet is something you either love or hate, but it has pleasant associations with high summer (it flowers from June to September) and appears in nice places, beside streams, fenland tracks and wood edges. It is a perennial and grows a metre or more in height. The leaves are large, separated into several pairs of saw-edged leaflets with a big three-lobed one at the tip. The flowers are small, 3 or 4mm across, six petalled and cream coloured. They grow in dense frothy heads, often attracting clouds of insects.

Meadowsweet

GOLDEN SAXIFRAGE

Chrysosplenium oppositifolium

The English name is grand and the scientific name is a mouthful, but the plant itself is small and tends to grow in damp shady places where it is not easy to appreciate. It is out from April to June, forming mats over wet rocks and the banks of streams, growing from a patchwork of creeping stems to a height of

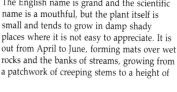

Golden saxifrage

5—10cm. The leaves are opposite and broad; at the top of the stem they give way to bracts and yellow calices which are 3—4mm in diameter. There are no petals.

A closely related species, the **alternate-leaved golden saxifrage**, *C. alternifolium*, has single rather than paired leaves and is much more local.

GREAT WILLOW-HERB *Epilobium hirsutum*

The leaves of most willow-herbs are the same shape as those of willow trees, hence the name. Those of the great willow-herb are lance shaped, stalkless, hairy and with a fine saw edge. They are usually about 10cm long, in opposite pairs up the stem. The plant grows up to 1.5m tall and the foliage can be very luxuriant, soft and downy. It sometimes dominates areas of marshland but is more likely to be seen in attractive stands along streams and rivers.

The flowers are out in July and August. They are about 2cm across and have four rose-pink petals, slightly notched as are those of all willow-herbs. At the heart of the flower is a fuzzy, cream-coloured, four-lobed stigma.

GIANT HOGWEED

Heracleum mantegazzianum

Everything about giant hogweed is larger than life. It grows to a prodigious 4m tall. Its stem is up to 10cm thick and its leaves are broad, deeply fingered and ragged edged, and a metre long. The great platforms or 'umbel' of small white flowers, like huge parasols, are about 50cm across. If size were not enough of

an intimidation, giant hogweed is also dangerous: brushing against the foliage on a sunny day produces rashes and blisters caused by chemicals in the plant reacting with vitamin D.

Giant hogweed flowers in July and August. It is a native of Asia and was introduced here as a garden plant, but it has colonised many river banks and waste places and is still spreading.

HEMLOCK WATER-DROPWORT
Oenanthe crocata

It is curious that hemlock water-dropwort is not more widely known, for it has been the cause of many tragedies. The roots look like parsnips and taste sweet; the stems are ridged and hollow and the leaves look like celery. Yet the whole plant contains a deadly poison, oenanthetoxin, fatal to horses and cattle as well as to humans.

The plant grows along streams and ditches, usually on neutral or slightly acid soils. It is a perennial and is in flower in July, by which time the foliage has grown a metre or more tall and is quite bushy. As in other members of the umbellifer or carrot family, the leaves are lacy, about 30cm long, but deeply fingered and then fingered again to produce the characteristic celery look.

The flower heads are split into about 20 dome-shaped umbels, each a tightly packed group of tiny white flowers on long rays. The umbels are not so platform or umbrella shaped as in most other members of the family such as cow parsley or pignut, and they look firm and sturdy. The entire plant looks innocuous and it is probably the absence of danger signs like red berries or a sinister smell that has made it a killer.

MARSH PENNYWORT
Hydrocotyle vulgaris

In bogs and marshes, wet woodland clearings and badly drained acid pastures, the round leaves of this little plant are very noticeable. If they were anything but green they would be

mistaken for toadstools. They are a few centimetres tall, round with a slightly crimped edge and a central stalk. Four or five cm across, they are too large to look like modern pennies, and are silky green in colour. If the flowers are present (not always the case) they will be found on short stems, growing in whorls of 4 or 5 at a time, each flower pink/green, no more than 1mm across. They appear in summer from June to August and are self-pollinated.

Wall pennywort, which grows in rock clefts and crevices in walls, is not closely related but has similar-shaped leaves.

GREAT WATER DOCK
Rumex hydrolapathum

People familiar with dock as a garden weed might shudder at the thought of a giant dock 2m tall, but great water dock is a plant of considerable elegance. It is found in fens and along river banks and lake shores, growing in silt either above or below the water.

The leaves are lance shaped, tapering at each end, and up to a metre in length. The flowers, out from July to September, are wind pollinated and therefore without showy petals since there is no need to attract insects.

Although small, only 6—8mm in length, these flowers are gathered together in dense branching heads, the colour — green turning a bright rust — contributing to the grandeur of the plant.

AMPHIBIOUS BISTORT
Polygonum amphibium

As the name implies this plant can live either on land or in water. It is a downy, long-stemmed perennial growing to 50 or 60cm. The leaves are oval, tapering to a blunt point. The two forms of the plant are rather different. The floating, aquatic form is large and has bigger leaves (up to 15cm long)

Amphibious bistort

which are hairy and have long stalks. It is found, sometimes in dense rafts, on sheltered lakes, ponds and derelict canals where the current is slight. The smaller land form is found on adjacent banks but also occurs in arable fields and waste places.

The flowers, out from July to September, are in a tight cylindrical spike, 3 or 4cm tall at the top of the stem. They are pink, stalkless, and 2 or 3mm long.

PURPLE LOOSESTRIFE *Lythrum salicaria*

Bushes of loosestrife make an impressive show along river banks and in fens and marshes, especially in July when the flowers are at their best.

Purple loosestrife is a tall downy perennial growing over a metre high. The leaves are about 6cm long, broad, lance shaped and stalkless, in opposite pairs or in trios up the main stem. The flowers are up to 15mm across, and are composed of six rather narrow petals, bright purple/red in colour, 12 stamens and a style. If the stamens are long the style is short and vice versa. Whorls of flowers grow from axils of leaf bracts, forming tall cylindrical spikes like candelabras on the branching tops of the stems.

YELLOW LOOSESTRIFE
Lysimachia vulgaris

Although similar in appearance and habitat to the purple loosestrife, this plant is more closely related to the primrose, as a detailed inspection of the flowers will reveal. It is an impressive plant, often over a metre tall. The leaves are about 10cm long, in opposite pairs or in groups of 3 or 4 up the stem, broad, lance shaped and covered with black dots.

The flowers are about 15cm across, the corolla composed of five broad, pointed lobes, yellow in colour, growing in branching spikes at the top of the stem. They are out in the months of July and August.

BOGBEAN *Menyanthes trifoliata*

An unfortunate name for a beautiful flower; in fact, the leaves do bear a resemblance to those of young broad-bean plants, being grey/green, long stalked and trifoliate.

Bogbean is a perennial growing from a creeping rootstock, often aquatic or rooted in saturated mud. It is particularly common in shallow, black, acid pools, but also occurs in bogs and marshes. The flowers, out in May and June, grow on a short spike up to 30cm tall. They are comparatively large, about 15mm across, with a five-lobed corolla, pink on the outside and pure white inside. Each lobe is recurved and has a fringe of white filaments which gives the whole plant an attractive feathery look.

BITTERSWEET *Solanum dulcamara*

Bittersweet belongs to the nightshade family, which also includes deadly nightshade and henbane. However, it is not quite so poisonous, and its genus, *Solanum*, also includes the potato. This is not to say that it is completely harmless for it contains the alkaloid solanine.

Bittersweet is a common scrambling or climbing perennial, found in many habitats but especially in marshy places. It grows up to 2m tall, depending on the supporting vegetation. The foliage is very like that of the potato, the leaves being up to 8mm long, broad with a pointed tip, heart or spear shaped with two lobes at the base. The flowers grow in loose drooping sprays and are composed of five pointed, recurved lobes, purple in colour, and a central column or narrowing tube of yellow stamens with a style in the middle. The flowers appear from June to September and are followed by oval berries, about 1cm long, which ripen from green to yellow to bright red.

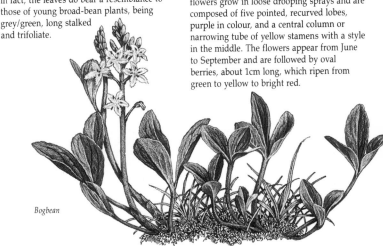

Bogbean

WATER FIGWORT *Scrophularia auriculata*
A tall herb of the waterside, more common in the south than the north, this plant is notable for the wings or ridges which form a frill up the edges of the square-shaped stem. This feature distinguishes it at once from the closely related common figwort (page 22). It is a perennial, up to a metre high, the stem often red or purple in colour. The leaves are about 10cm long, oval but tapering slightly to a blunt tip, smooth and with an even, round-toothed edge.

The flowers resemble those of common figwort and grow in clusters from the leaf axils towards the top of the stem. They have a dull-purple, berry-shaped corolla with a narrow opening and a double-lobed roof, and are pollinated by wasps in the months of August and September.

MONKEY FLOWER *Mimulus guttatus*
Many plants and animals have been introduced into the British countryside, by accident or design. Monkey flower came from the western United States as a garden flower but escaped over 150 years ago and is now completely naturalised along rivers in the north and west of Britain.

The foliage is hairy above, smooth below, with leaves up to 7cm long, heavily toothed and oval with a pointed tip. They grow in opposite pairs up the stem. The plant usually forms small clumps, the stems up to 50cm tall but usually less where it is rooted in mud or pebbles on the exposed shores of burns and becks.

The flowers, out from July to September, are large, composed of a five-toothed green calyx and a bright-yellow corolla about 3cm across. This is shaped like a foxglove (page 22) with a two-lobed upper lip and a much larger three-lobed lower lip. The mouth of the corolla tube is nearly closed by a raised area or 'palate'; this is usually marked with red spots and sometimes the lower lobes are spotted too. If all the corolla lobes carry large red blotches and the mouth of the corolla tube is open, you are probably not looking at monkey flower at all but at **blood-drop-emlets**, *M. luteus*, another naturalised species, this time coming from South America.

Monkey flower with detail of flower head

BROOKLIME *Veronica beccabunga*

Brooklime is a speedwell, but although the flowers are typically blue (see germander speedwell, page 43) and appear throughout the summer, they are rather small, 7 or 8mm across, and not always very conspicuous. The most obvious thing about this plant of streams and marshes is its fleshy stems and leaves, and it comes as little surprise that it was once recommended as a salad crop and as a cure or preventative for scurvy.

Brooklime forms a patchwork of creeping stems which root in mud, then send up flowering stems to a height of 20 or 30cm. The leaves are smooth, about 5cm long, and oval with a slightly serrated edge. They grow in opposite pairs; the flowers are carried on paired racemes or branching spikes which grow from the leaf axils. The corolla is deep blue, composed of four flattened lobes of which the lowest lobe is the smallest. As with other speedwells, a pair of stamens projects outwards like mouse whiskers.

The scientific name is, for once, easy to remember, either because it sounds like a distinguished South American dancer or because it suggests the plant bungs up becks — which it does!

WATER MINT *Mentha aquatica*

Peppermint originates from a cross between the garden herb spearmint and wild water mint. The smell of the latter plant is not so intense but is very refreshing when encountered on a riverside walk.

Water mint is a member of the labiate or dead-nettle family and shares many of their features; the stem is square in cross section, the leaves are opposite, broad and bluntly toothed, and the flowers grow in dense whorls or tufts in the axils of the upper 2 or 3 pairs of leaves and at the top of the stem. The individual flowers are mauve or lilac coloured, very small, with an open, four-lobed corolla and projecting stamens.

The whole plant is hairy and is inclined to turn a bronze/purple colour, making it look a little mildewed. It grows to a height of 40 or 50cm along streams and in marshes and ditches, and is in flower from July to October.

SKULLCAP *Scutellaria galericulata*

A *galerum* was a leather skull-helmet worn by Roman soldiers, and the name *galericulata* was translated into English in the 18th century to give us the term skullcap. To find out why the name seemed appropriate to herbalists you have to look closely at the calyx at the base of the flower. This is unusual in that it is separated into two lips, the upper one of which has a bump or lobe towards its base. It is this that inspired comparison with ancient headgear and gave us the plant's Latin name.

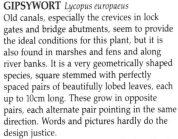

Skullcap with detail of flower head

Skullcap is an attractive blue-flowered perennial of wet dykes, river banks and canal towpaths, out from mid- to late summer. It is usually quite short, 20—30cm, with bluntly toothed, lance-shaped leaves up to 5cm long. The flowers grow from the upper leaf axils or bracts, always in pairs facing the same way on the stem rather than in opposite directions. The calyx is short but the corolla is long and slightly arched, the whole flower measuring 20—25mm.

GIPSYWORT *Lycopus europaeus*

Old canals, especially the crevices in lock gates and bridge abutments, seem to provide the ideal conditions for this plant, but it is also found in marshes and fens and along river banks. It is a very geometrically shaped species, square stemmed with perfectly spaced pairs of beautifully lobed leaves, each up to 10cm long. These grow in opposite pairs, each alternate pair pointing in the same direction. Words and pictures hardly do the design justice.

The flowers are very small; the calyx is green with long teeth, the corolla is about 3mm long, four lobed and white with purple dots, looking pink from a distance. The flowers grow from the leaf axils, grouped tightly around the stem in neat whorls. Gipsywort is a perennial, growing up to a metre tall, flowering from June to September. When crushed it yields a black dye, once used as a face paint by wandering vagabonds in an attempt to pass themselves off as gipsies.

WATER FORGET-ME-NOT
Myosotis scorpioides

Forget-me-nots are beautiful in their simplicity, but they can be hard work to tell apart. Water forget-me-not usually grows close enough to a stream or pond to have its rhizomes wet. It has alternate, blunt, stemless leaves and a branching stem 20—30cm tall, topped by a curved head of pink buds that open into pure-blue flowers. These have a

Comfrey

toothed calyx, the teeth less than half the total length of the calyx, and a five-lobed corolla up to 10mm across.

A closely related species, **creeping forget-me-not**, *M. secunda*, grows alongside more peaty, acidic waters and has slightly longer calyx teeth. Both plants are in flower throughout the summer.

COMFREY *Symphytum officinale*

Comfrey is a healing herb, its leaves still widely used in a hot poultice for bruises and sprains. The presence of the chemical allantoin may be responsible for the curative effect. Over a metre tall, it is a very rough and bristly perennial plant with a winged or ridged stem and lance-shaped leaves up to 25cm long. The flowers grow in a curled, nodding head and are composed of a toothed calyx 8mm long and a corolla tube, white, mauve or purple, about 16mm long.

Comfrey grows in most damp places and is out in May and June. Bavarians cook its leaves in batter and call it *schwartzwurz*.

VALERIAN *Valeriana officinalis*

During and after World War I valerian tea, made from an infusion of the roots and rhizomes, was a popular relaxant or sedative. That it is gaining favour again perhaps reflects a return to the belief that nature's remedies are best.

Valerian is a rather slender herb of marshes and overgrown verges, growing to over a metre in height. The leaves are in opposite pairs, up to 20cm long, narrow and separated into roughly toothed leaflets. The flowers are small, about 4mm across, pale pink, with a five-lobed corolla tube and rather long stamens. They are out from June to August and are carried in dense 'umbels' or umbrella-shaped flower heads. The dry foliage of valerian is supposed to be irresistible to cats.

BUTTERBUR *Petasites hybridus*
The giant, mysterious rhubarb-shaped leaves of butterbur dominate many streamsides and wet woodland clearings during the summer months, by which time the flowers will have long gone.

Butterbur is a composite, a member of the daisy family, and the individual flower heads are of the familiar basic structure with a core of tubular florets, pink or purple in colour. However, the flower heads are very short stalked and are gathered into a club-shaped spike on a thick stem which usually only just rises clear of the ground. This is in March or April; the leaves appear as the spike is dying back and they continue to grow and grow until they are a metre tall and nearly a metre across. They are long stalked, downy, round or heart shaped with a toothed edge. After a few weeks, slug holes and heavy rain will have reduced them to a tattered remnant, but they still make an ideal adventure playground for children. Years ago the leaves were used to wrap butter.

HEMP AGRIMONY
Eupatorium cannabinum
Very common in marshes and fens, and among tall roadside herbage, hemp agrimony is not related to hemp or to agrimony and is actually a composite or daisy. It grows from a rootstock and its downy stem can be more than a metre tall, branching only at the top to form many-flowered heads. At first glance the individual heads do not resemble those of a daisy; the florets have short tubes and long stamens and styles. There are only 5 or 6 florets to each head, but since the heads are so closely grouped the total effect is of a bushy, pale raspberry-coloured umbel or dome-shaped platform about 15cm across.

The leaves growing from the base of the plant have long stalks and are broadest towards the tip. Those growing on the stem, in opposite pairs, are stalkless, trifoliate and toothed. Hemp agrimony is out in the late summer and is very attractive to insects.

Top right:
Sea holly
Top left:
Sea sandwort
Middle left:
Alexanders

Carline thistle

Above: *Burnet rose*
Left: *Thrift*

Fumitory

Heartsease

Common poppy

Spring squill

Chickweed

Broad-leaved
willow-herb

Rosebay willow-herb

Greater plantain

Scarlet pimpernel

Common toadflax

Red dead-nettle

Creeping
thistle

White dead-
nettle

Oxford ragwort

Groundsel

Daisy

SNEEZEWORT *Achillea ptarmica*
This plant is neither a cure for nor a cause of sneezing, though it confused one famous herbalist, Gerard, into blaming it for the latter. Sneezewort is closely related to yarrow (page 51). It is found in marshy places, in meadows and beside streams, but it is most common in the northern uplands where the soil is acidic. It grows from a creeping rootstock to a height of 30—40cm. The leaves are simple, slim and lance shaped, 5 or 6cm long, with a finely toothed edge.

Sneezewort is out in July and August. The flower heads resemble those of other daisies, with white ray florets encircling a platform of pale grey-green disc florets. The leaves are more than twice the size of those of yarrow but do not appear in such profusion and there are usually only a few out on the plant at a time.

MARSH THISTLE *Cirsium palustre*
Thistles can be majestic plants. A stand of marsh thistles, as tall as a man, their foliage suffused with purple and their flowers alive with bumblebees and butterflies, is worth more than a passing glance.

Like most of the larger 'plume' thistles, this species is a biennial, passing winter as a flat rosette of leaves before sending up a tall flowering stem in its second summer. The stem is downy or covered in a fine mat of cottony hairs, and has shiny wings or ridges all the way up. The leaves are heavily lobed, each lobe more or less transformed into an armoury of spines. The base leaves are similar and not quite so threatening, but are still an adequate deterrent to grazing animals. The flower heads grow at the top of the stem and are gathered into a tight knot or cluster. They measure about 2cm long and less than 2cm across. Each head has an outer covering of pointed purplish bracts and a shaving-brush of florets, usually rich purple but sometimes almost white (especially on plants growing on high ground). Marsh thistle is a plant of fens, wet grassland and woodland verges and is in flower from July to September.

WATER PLANTAIN
Alisma plantago-aquatica

It takes a good imagination to see how this plant came to be called a plantain; it is in no way related but the leaves are supposed to resemble those of ribwort plantain. It is an emergent or semi-aquatic plant, up to a metre tall, and the slender stem carries whorls or tiers of fine branches which divide into long stalks. At the ends of these stalks are three-petalled pale-pink flowers, up to 1cm across, which only open in the afternoon. The flowering season is June to August.

Water plantain with detail of flower head

The leaves are up to 20cm long, lance shaped and with parallel unribbed veins. They grow from the base of the plant on tall rigid stalks. Water plantain is found in the mud of ponds or slow-moving rivers and canals. In America the leaves were rubbed on to rattlesnake bites.

YELLOW IRIS *Iris pseudacorus*

The dramatic flowers of yellow iris, the original fleur-de-lys, grace marshes and swamps from late May to July. The leaves are sword shaped, up to 25mm wide, and a metre tall. The flower stems grow to the same

Yellow iris

height, producing a spathe or sheath containing 2 or 3 furled flowers. These open in turn, one after the other. In their full glory they measure up to 10cm across, with three spoon-shaped curled lobes or outer segments and a group of smaller inner segments including petal-like stigmas.

Black dye can be made from the thick submerged rhizomes and the seeds have been roasted and ground as a substitute for coffee.

NORTHERN MARSH ORCHID
Dactyloriza purpurella

There are two marsh orchids, very closely related, one in the north *(D. purpurella)* and one in the south *(D. praetermissa)*. They are out in June and July, in meadows and damp, lime-rich marshes. Northern marsh orchid is 15—20cm tall, with broad lance-shaped leaves, 6 or 7 in number, unspotted or with just a few large blotches near the tip. The flowers are in a dense broad spike and have a diamond-shaped lower lip; they are a remarkable deep purple in colour. In comparison, the southern marsh orchid is taller, usually 30 or 40cm, with more leaves and a conical spike of pale-purple flowers.

COAST

*V*ery few flowering plants can survive in salt water but above the high tide marks things are different, even if conditions may at times seem daunting. The power of the sea, its ability to destroy and create, is not confined to occasional floods and tempests. There is a constant process of erosion and deposition. Mud, sand and shingle move with the wind and with the tides, especially during the winter months. Thus plants survive by having firm roots or by completing their cycle between seasonal storms. Even during the summer, cliffs can crumble and sand can be blown away. More especially at this time of year there is the problem of drying out: rain drains very quickly through sand and shingle and many coastal plants have succulent stems or leaves in which they can store water.

Britain has a long and beautiful coastline and its habitats are varied. Sand dunes, shingle beaches, cliffs and river outfalls may all occur within sight of a single seafront hotel. For more extensive and dramatic examples of coastal habitats it is useful to open a map and find places away from civilisation. This is easier said than done in the south, but between Kent and Dorset there are some majestic chalk and limestone headlands alternating with sandy bays and shingle ridges. The east coast is noted for its estuaries and mudflats, whilst the north and west have rocky shores and towering cliffs.

Some of these habitats are under pressure through recreation and reclamation. Sand dunes are especially fragile: they are created by drifts of sand and can easily be damaged by trampling and digging so that the wind breaks through the covering of vegetation. Within a few months they may have vanished.

Most coastal habitats have an unexpected beginning and a dramatic end. The fact that they owe their existence to the elements rather than to human influences makes their wild flowers all the more special.

YELLOW-HORNED POPPY

Glaucium flavum

Exposed shingle beaches are the preferred habitat for the unique and exotic-looking yellow-horned poppy. It is a biennial or short-lived perennial, surviving the winter as a rosette of leaves and growing in the spring to a height of 60—70cm. The stems tend to branch outwards and upwards, establishing a rounded profile and cushioning the plant from buffeting winds. The leaves are grey-green, broadly lobed and leathery, either growing from the base or clasped around the stem. From June to September the flowers are produced; these are of the usual poppy shape but are large, up to 9cm across, and bright yellow. The petals soon fall and an immensely long curved seed case or capsule develops.

SEA BEET *Beta vulgaris*

A plant of sea walls and shingle ridges, sea beet can grow an impressive metre or more in height. It has a simple tap root from which rise fleshy red-striped stems and heart-shaped leaves. The shiny upper-stem leaves are more variable, sometimes diamond shaped and red tinged. At the top of the stem are tall spikes of tiny green flowers, pollinated by the wind and out from July to September.

Over the centuries, and after much improvement, beet has become one of the most important root crops in the world. It is difficult to believe that this maritime plant is the ancestor of the mangel wurzel (the name is German for 'famine-root'), beetroot and sugar beet.

WILD CABBAGE *Brassica oleracea*

This is not a common plant but, as the ancestor of the brussel sprout and broccoli, not to mention the cultivated cabbage, it is a species of classical distinction. It is an inhabitant of chalk and limestone sea cliffs in the south and west, rarely elsewhere, and may either be a native plant or possibly a Roman introduction.

Wild cabbage is a perennial with a tap root and a thickened stem, from which rise the broad, oblong leaves. These are lobed at the base, fleshy and grey-green in colour. The flowers are out from May to August and are carried on a tall, narrow spike. They are four petalled, pale yellow and 3 or 4cm wide.

Sea beet

SEA ROCKET *Cakile maritima*

A long, narrow tap root reduces the risk of sea rocket drying out or being blown away on the shifting foreshore sands that are its usual habitat. It is an annual, its seeds carried on the drift line, and is found all round the coast of Britain. The branching stems grow outwards and upwards, to a height of 20—40cm. As with many other seashore plants, the leaves, 3—6cm long, are thick and

succulent and are rather narrow and heavily lobed, particularly those growing low on the stem. The flowers are pink or white, four petalled and about 10cm across, in loose, many-flowered heads at the top of the stem. They are out from June to August and are visited by various insects, especially bumblebees which must travel some distance from more flowery habitats.

Exposed clumps of sea rocket, caught against the wind, soon accumulate piles of sand around them. Every now and then these last long enough to be colonised by marram grass, thus starting a cycle of dune formation. From such small beginnings whole islands can evolve.

SCURVY GRASS *Cochlearia officinalis*

We now know that vitamin C is vital to our diet, but 2 or 3 centuries ago it must have seemed miraculous that an untidy, bitter-tasting plant of the seashore could prevent scurvy. Sailors took sackfuls of dried scurvy grass on their long voyages and it was generally available, either fresh or in a preserved state, until the introduction of oranges and lemons.

Swathes of scurvy grass flower in summer on most rocky headlands and saltmarshes and are especially luxuriant on the west coast. It is not a grass, being related to cabbage and charlock (page 103) and therefore a crucifer. It is a biennial or perennial, 10—50cm tall, the stems growing outwards and upwards to a loose head of white four-petalled flowers. These are about 9mm across. When the first flowers have been fertilised the stem and stalks elongate so that more flowers can appear at the top whilst allowing space for the disc-shaped seed cases to develop. The leaves of scurvy grass are fleshy and smooth, long stalked and heart shaped at the base but stalkless and triangular or oval on the stem.

SEA CAMPION *Silene maritima*

Sea campion appears as large, loosely formed cushions on cliffs and rocky shores. Its leaves are lance shaped, grey-green, rather fleshy and 2 or 3cm long. The flowering stems are 10—25cm tall with a loose head of 1—4 flowers which are out from June to August. These are large and have a very bulky, pink/purple cylindrical calyx and five broad, deeply notched white petals. The whole flower measures up to 25mm across.

Although it seems tied to the coast, sea campion also grows at the top of mountains. Presumably, shared factors between these habitats, such as a reduction in the competition for light, work to the advantage of the plant.

SEA SANDWORT *Honkenya peploides*

What may look from a distance to be bare green/yellow tide lines on sandy or pebbly beaches often turn out to be carpets of sea sandwort. It is a creeping perennial with very short erect stems 10—15cm tall, upon which are arranged a closely packed sequence of very fleshy leaves, each 10—15mm long,

oval and pointed. These grow in alternate pairs so that the whole plant looks rigid and geometrical.

The flowers are dull, 6—10mm in diameter, with five pale-green or off-white petals. They are out from May to September and are succeeded by more conspicuous green seed cases containing dark-brown, pear-shaped seeds.

FROSTED ORACHE *Atriplex laciniata*

This is a plant of the high tide mark on sandy beaches. It is an annual able to grow and seed between spring tides and survive salt sprays, but likely to be blown or washed away in unexpected gales.

Frosted orache has a buff or pink stem up to 30cm long, always sprawling over the surface so that the leaves often seem to be growing directly out of the sand. The leaves are diamond shaped, with a slightly lobed or angled edge, and are fleshy with a dusty or grainy grey surface. The flowers are tiny, in spikes or in leaf axils. They are pollinated by the wind and are out in late summer.

Sea sandwort

GLASSWORT *Salicornia spp.*

If it were in a desert, you might think glasswort was a sort of cactus. It has no obvious leaves and the stem and branches are succulent. Green or bronze in colour, they are separated into slightly bulging segments, each having a pair of triangular lobes which are actually the modified leaves. The flowers are little more than paired blips of red anthers appearing on the upper segments in August and September.

There are several different species of glasswort, mostly annuals between 10 and 30cm in height growing candelabra-style in saltings and mudflats. Beds of glasswort were once harvested and burned to provide the glass-making industry with soda from the ashes. The plant was also picked as a salad crop or for pickling and is still sold as 'samphire' in some East Anglian markets.

STORK'S-BILL *Erodium cicutarium*

Once coastal dunes have become 'fixed' they are colonised by a diverse group of flowers. Among these is stork's-bill, an annual related to the crane's-bills, but with its leaves separated into deeply toothed leaflets. It usually spreads outwards rather than upwards, to 30 or 40cm in length. The flowers, a loose arrangement of 6 or 7 per head, appear from June to September. They are about 14mm across and have five pink/purple petals which soon fall to reveal a long straight 'beak'. This then splits spirally to allow the seeds to disperse. The entire plant is covered with silvery, slightly sticky hairs.

WESTERN GORSE *Ulex gallii*

Blazing golden thickets of low-growing gorse on western coasts in the late summer are likely to be this species rather than common gorse (page 58). It rarely grows more than a metre tall, its flowers are smaller, up to 12mm long, and its thorns are not heavily furrowed.

Otherwise the main difference between the two plants is the flowering season, with western gorse in blossom from July to October, the only time of the year when common gorse is not out. There is an old saying that kissing is in season as long as gorse is in flower.

A third species, **dwarf gorse**, *U. minor*, occurs on heathland in the south and east, and is in flower from July to August.

BURNET ROSE *Rosa pimpinellifolia*

Most wild roses differ in points of detail, but the lovely burnet rose is quite unlike any other. It is the most likely species to be encountered on dunes or coastal heaths and can either grow as a single shrub or spread by suckers to form prickly, low-growing tangles. The branching stems are covered with fine straight prickles and bristles and are between 30 and 50cm tall. The flowers are out from May to July. They are large, 30—40mm across, and similar in structure to other roses with five slightly notched petals, but cream or white rather than pink. They usually grow singly at the top of the stem and have a very beautiful scent. By comparison the foliage is less distinctive; the leaves are composed of 7 or 9 small leaflets each about 1cm long and finely toothed. The common name refers to the similarity of the leaves to those of salad Burnet (page 40).

BITING STONECROP *Sedum acre*

Among all the obscure yet delightfully eccentric names the British have used for wild flowers there can be few so evocative as 'welcome-home-husband-though-never-so-drunk'. This was at one time a more widespread name for *Sedum acre* than 'biting stonecrop' or 'wallpepper', both of which refer to the plant's peppery taste and habit of growth. The plant probably got the longer,

Biting stonecrop

older name because it thrives on the stone roofs of old porches and would have been the first thing a cottager saw when he was helped across the threshold after a night on the tiles.

There are, in fact, several species of stonecrop of which two, biting stonecrop and **English stonecrop,** *S. anglicum,* are common and coastal though they are also found on rocks and walls inland. They are very short, mat-forming perennials, evergreen with succulent oval leaves 3—5mm long. English stonecrop grows to about 5cm tall and has reddish stems and leaves and white, five-petalled flowers. Biting stonecrop grows to 10cm and has yellow flowers. It has a shorter flowering season, June and July rather than May to August, but it is probably better known because of its brighter colour and the fact that it is more widespread inland.

SEA HOLLY *Eryngium maritimum*

The resemblance to holly is in the leaves, which are waxy, grey-green and prickly. Sea holly is a perennial of sandy beaches, growing to a height of 40 or 50cm. The leaves growing from the base or roots are fan shaped with long stalks, whilst those on the stem are typically holly shaped and stemless. They are all finely veined and have sharp spines. The flowers grow in dense round heads comprising spiky bracts and bright-blue flowers, each about 8mm across. They are out from June to September.

Although it looks, and feels, like a thistle, sea holly is an umbellifer, related to cow parsley and carrot. The roots were once candied with sugar and sold as 'eryngo'.

ALEXANDERS *Smyrnium olusatrum*

The Romans are credited with introducing many Mediterranean herbs which are now roadside weeds. Alexanders, related to angelica, is a member of the carrot family. Its blanched lower shoots were once a popular winter vegetable and it is quite likely that it was the Romans who brought it here nearly 2,000 years ago. Today it is common on cliffs and along road verges near the coast.

Alexanders is a biennial, growing over a metre tall, and has shiny, dark-green foliage composed of numerous long-stalked leaves split into small diamond-shaped leaflets. The flowers are out from April to June; they are small and yellow, less than 2mm across, gathered in round umbels growing at the top of stems or from the leaf axils.

ROCK SAMPHIRE *Crithmum maritimum*

The leaves of rock samphire were, and still are, collected for pickling in a similar way to glasswort, sometimes known as marsh samphire (page 95). Otherwise the two plants are totally dissimilar and are unrelated.

Rock samphire, or 'semper' as it is often known, is another seaside umbellifer or carrot, like Alexanders. However, it is only 20 or 30cm tall and has short-stalked, blue-green leaves cut into long fleshy leaflets. The flowers are yellow and about 2mm across, in umbels or flat heads about 5cm in diameter. It is found on cliffs and rocky coasts from June to August.

SEA SPURGE *Euphorbia paralias*

Spurges have an unusual structure in which the flowers have neither petals nor sepals but are carried in green dishes of bracts in a flattened head or umbel. Each dish (or 'cyathium') is composed of four lobes and contains four yellow glands and a group of small single-stamened male flowers and a solitary female flower.

Sea spurge, in flower from July to October, is found on dunes and stable sandy beaches in the south and west. It has a typical spurge flower head, an umbel with between 6 and 8 rays, but like many other coastal plants it is more succulent than inland species. It is a perennial, with trailing or upright reddish stems growing to a height of 30 or 40cm. The leaves are oval, up to 2cm long, overlapping up the stem. They are stemless, concave, fleshy, and of a waxy grey-green colour.

Like all other spurges this species bleeds a white sticky sap when it is damaged. Although the foliage is bitter and poisonous to most animals, it is the foodplant of one of Britain's rarest and most beautiful hawk-moths, the spurge hawk.

SEA LAVENDER *Limonium vulgare*

Grey mudflats can turn a bright hazy purple as drifts of sea lavender shimmer in August sunshine and early autumn breezes. If they are growing in abundance, a few flowers will not be missed; they make good winter decorations because they dry well and keep their colour for months after picking.

Sea lavender is a perennial with a short woody rootstock, sending up a rosette of lance-shaped leaves from the shrubby bases of the previous year's growth. These leaves are long stalked, broadest towards the tip, and are 5—10cm long. The flowers grow in rows or clusters on curved branches, at the top of thin leafless stems 10—30cm tall. The individual flowers are small and have a purple/blue corolla about 8mm across. When this withers and falls, the papery calyx, pale purple in colour, persists and holds nectar which continues to attract insects.

There are several very similar species of sea lavender of which two, the common **sea lavender**, *L. vulgare*, and the **lax-flowered sea lavender**, *L. humile*, are found on saltmarshes all round the English coast.

THRIFT *Armeria maritima*

Clumps of thrift, shivering and dancing against an onshore breeze, are the essence of sea cliffs and islands. Thrift is a short, cushion-forming perennial with rosettes of grass-like leaves up to 10cm long. The flower stems are about 20cm high, leafless and downy, with a dense head of pink flowers at the tip. These are composed of a toothed, five-lobed calyx tube and a pink corolla about 8mm across. The entire head is about 2cm in diameter, protected by a papery case of bracts or scales, the lowest of which form a purple/brown sheath or tube around the top of the stem. Thrift is in flower from late spring to early autumn but is at its best around the midsummer period.

Thrift

SEA MILKWORT *Glaux maritima*

A short, creeping succulent of grassy saltmarshes and salt-sprayed rocky crevices, this plant is related to the primrose rather than to the true milkworts. The stem is between 10 and 30cm long and bears opposite pairs of blunt fleshy leaves, grey or blue/green in colour, up to 12mm long. The flowers, growing singly from the leaf axils, are out from May to August. They are stalkless, have a five-lobed pink calyx (no petals or corolla lobes) and measure about 5mm across.

Sea milkwort, which is also known as black saltwort, is found only in places where there is salt.

VIPERS BUGLOSS *Echium vulgare*

An eye-catching combination of blue and pink flowers against hoary green foliage makes vipers bugloss one of the easiest of plants to identify on coastal dunes, shingle and on dry limestone soils inland. It is a biennial with hairy strap- or lance-shaped leaves, flowering from June to September and growing nearly a metre tall in sheltered places. On the upper part of the bristly stem are a series of leaf-like bracts; from the axils of these develop curled clusters of pink buds. These open into flowers about 16mm long. The corolla is funnel shaped, bright blue, and five lobed with the upper lobes larger than the lower ones. From the corolla extend four long pink stamens and a simple stigma.

SEA ASTER *Aster tripolium*
Patches of sea aster often grow amid the flotsam of the spring tide line, looking like fugitive clumps of Michaelmas daisy. In fact the two plants belong to the same genus and have similar flowers. The flower heads are strongly scented, up to 2cm across with yellow disc florets and purple/pink ray florets. They are out from July to September.

Sea aster is a perennial of saltmarshes and sometimes of rocky clefts close to the sea. It has smooth branching stems, usually grows about 30cm tall (sometimes much more if conditions allow) and has fleshy, lance-shaped leaves.

CARLINE THISTLE *Carlina vulgaris*
Carline thistle is at home on rabbit-cropped coastal grassland and dunes or on open downland. The delicate tracery of its downy, purple-flushed bracts makes it a lovely plant, but virtually untouchable because of its spines and prickles.

It is a biennial, growing to 20 or 30cm. The leaves are yellow/green, lance shaped and edged by prickles. The purple stem branches candelabra-fashion towards the top, each branch ending in a dense head of prickly outer bracts enclosing a ring of longer orange inner bracts. These resemble the ray florets of other composite flowers but are papery and shiny. The actual florets are purple/red but are partly obscured in a mat of orange bristles. Carline thistle is out from July to October, at the end of which the bleached flower heads, 3 or 4cm across, resemble everlasting flowers in winter decorations.

SPRING SQUILL *Scilla verna*
Pale-blue drifts of squill are characteristic of grassy cliff tops. There are two species, spring and **autumn squill**, *S. autumnalis*, flowering at each end of the summer. They are typical members of the lily family growing from a bulb and with grass-like leaves. They produce a single flower stalk about 10 or 15cm tall. The flowers are fragrant, violet/blue with six pointed lobes or segments. Spring squill has a rounded flower head and bracts beneath the flowers whilst autumn squill has a more elongated head and has no bracts. Both species are local with a western bias, but are abundant where they occur.

Spring squill

URBAN WASTELAND AND GARDENS

*E*verything made by mankind is a part of nature, and most natural habitats in Britain have been affected by human influence. Although it is difficult to accept that concrete and clay are suitable settings for wild flowers there is no logical reason why they should not be there. Ideal growing conditions abound as new plots of land are cleared and old buildings are ripped down. Victorian gutters, railways lines, motorway embankments and derelict gardens all offer scope for colonisation.

The most striking aspects of urban life, for plants as for humans, are that the pace is fast and the population cosmopolitan. Habitats are created as a by-product of change. Annual weeds are particularly successful, and able to establish themselves in a trice when a patch of ground is uncovered. If the space is available for more than a season or two, aggressive perennials will succeed the annuals: the make-up of communities is never as stable as it is in other habitats.

It is difficult to tell where most urban weeds first came from. Clearly they have not had the time necessary to evolve in situ. Some made the transition from hills and coasts where they were colonisers of scree and bare mud. Others arrived in the wake of invading armies or as stowaways on trading ships. Seeds are very inconspicuous. A large number — perhaps more than we imagine — were deliberately planted as crops or medicinal herbs, and were brought here from Mediterranean countries. Thus an old allotment can be interpreted as an exciting story of Roman invasion, medieval famine and jet-setting opportunism.

There is no doubt that a knowledge of flowers is often inspired by an interest in things close to home, and this section will contain weeds familiar, by sight at least, to most people. In the plant world there is not really such a thing as a weed — it is merely a term to describe a plant growing out of place where it is not wanted. For this reason a rose can be called a weed while dandelion and dock can be accepted as attractive perennial herbs, doing no harm and bringing a spark of colour to dull wastes.

CREEPING BUTTERCUP
Ranunculus repens

Gardeners with little knowledge of wild flowers know creeping buttercup only too well. It spreads efficiently, sending out long runners which root and produce new plants. These appear in all sorts of places — in

lawns, between paving stones, anywhere it is not wanted. It is an especially common plant on clay soils, in waste places, damp fields and in woodland. The flowers resemble those of meadow buttercup (page 34) and are out from May to August. They are 2—3cm across, five petalled and glossy. Beneath the petals are five hairy sepals. These soon fall off causing some confusion because the shape of the sepals is used as an identification feature for buttercups. Thus, no sepals at all usually means the plant is creeping buttercup.

The base leaves are long stalked and divided into three heavily toothed lobes, the middle lobe extending beyond the other two. The stem is 20—50cm tall, hairy and branched into 4 or 5 furrowed flower stalks.

COMMON POPPY *Papaver rhoeas*

Poppies have always grown in cornfields and it is still possible to drive down a country lane in June or July and be dazzled by a sea of dancing red flowers. In addition to arable fields, the common poppy is found on all types of waste ground, wherever the soil has been disturbed to allow the tiny seeds to germinate.

Common or field poppy is an annual, 20—50cm tall, with deeply fingered and toothed leaves and a slender bristly stem. The flowers are enclosed at first in a pair of green sepals. These are shed as the crumpled petals expand, two unequal pairs of silky red petals opening out to produce a flower head up to 10cm across. Despite its size, the poppy is fragile and the petals quickly fall — the perfect symbol for Remembrance Day.

Poppy seed capsules are beautifully designed pepperpot structures, dispersing seeds by shaking them out from a series of holes. The common poppy has a smooth oval capsule with a flat top; other species can be recognised by their long smooth capsule (**long-headed poppy**, *P. dubium*) or long bristly capsule (**prickly poppy**, *P. argemone*).

FUMITORY *Fumaria officinalis*

A common annual weed of dry, sandy or chalky soils, fumitory is a delicate sprawling plant, growing to a height of 10—20cm and flowering throughout the summer.

The leaves are divided into grey/green leaflets, which are themselves finely lobed. The flower stems grow opposite to the leaf stalks, displaying 20 or 30 short-stemmed flowers per head. The individual flowers are narrow and tube shaped, about 8mm long, composed of a pair of tiny sepals and two pairs of petals, waxy pink with a smoky-purple tip. Although fumitory produces nectar it is rarely visited by insects and is almost always self-pollinated.

CHARLOCK *Sinapis arvensis*

As with other troublesome arable weeds, charlock can suddenly appear in profusion when a field is ploughed, the seeds lying dormant for decades until conditions are again favourable. It is a member of the cabbage family, an annual growing to a height of 30—60cm, with coarsely toothed oval or spear-shaped leaves up to 15cm long, and a bristly stem. The flowers are four petalled, yellow, about 16mm across, in a stalked head at the tip of the stem. This elongates to allow the seed pods to develop whilst more flowers are produced from the tip.

Like nettles and other marginal vegetables, charlock was welcome in Ireland and the Western Isles in times of famine.

SHEPHERD'S PURSE
Capsella bursa-pastoris

An annual weed, sometimes surviving through a mild winter and into a second summer, shepherd's purse grows virtually anywhere and flowers all year round.

Shepherd's purse with part of stem and flower head

The leaves are lance shaped, usually heavily lobed, in a low rosette. From the middle of the rosette rises an erect stem, sometimes branched, at the top of which is a cluster of small four-petalled white flowers. Beneath the flowers the stem elongates (as in the charlock and scurvy grass, page 93), so that by early winter the stem may be 20 or 30cm tall with a series of heart-shaped seed cases borne on lateral stalks. These seed cases split easily to release a cache of minuscule seeds.

MIGNONETTE *Reseda lutea*

Mignonette and **weld** (*R. luteola*) belong to
their own small family and are rather similar,
though the latter is taller and has lance-
shaped leaves and a narrower flower head.

Mignonette is a short-lived perennial of
disturbed ground, usually where the soil is
chalky. It forms bushes to a height of up to
75cm, the leaves heavily cut into lobes then
divided again so that the foliage often seems
an untidy jumble. The branching stems are
ridged and ascend to spikes of short-stalked
flowers. These are six petalled (with four
petals deeply toothed), yellow and about
6mm in diameter. They are out from June to
August. Weld, or dyer's rocket, used to be
cultivated for green and yellow dyes.

HEARTSEASE *Viola tricolor*

The romantic common name is of Victorian
vintage; a more recent alternative is wild
pansy. Heartsease is an annual weed of arable
fields and other open ground, growing to a
height of 15—40cm. The leaves are oval,
narrowing further up the stem, and bluntly
toothed. Beneath the leaf bases there are ruffs
of lobed leafy growths called stipules. The
flowers, about 2cm across, grow singly on
long slender stalks rising
from the leaf axils.

They are out from May to September and are
composed of five unequal petals, the upper
pair flat and mostly purple, the side pair
paler, sometimes white or yellowish. The
rather short lower petal is more or less
yellow, extending back into a spur which
contains the nectar.

CHICKWEED *Stellaria media*

Boiled chickweed is unexpectedly palatable. It
is such a universal weed of vegetable gardens
that it seems somehow appropriate that it
should be edible.

    Chickweed is an annual, flowering all
year, growing by means of trailing, round
stems; these are edged on one side only by a
row of fine hairs. The leaves are about 20mm
long, oval with a pointed tip, silky smooth
and dark green, in opposite pairs along the
stem. The flowers grow in terminal clusters or
from leaf axils. They are rather small,
composed of five green, pointed sepals and
five slightly shorter, deeply divided white
petals. The stamens, up to eight to a flower,
have red anthers.

Chickweed

FAT HEN *Chenopodium album*

Seeds of fat hen and heartsease were in the meal given to Tollund man before he was killed and thrown into a Danish bog 2,000 years ago. In fact, archaeological analysis has shown fat hen to be one of the most widespread of ancient foods, yet it has not been taken into modern cultivation and is now little more than a weed of waste ground and allotments.

Fat hen is a rather nondescript annual, usually 50—60cm tall. It has a reddish stem and diamond-shaped leaves, irregularly and bluntly toothed and grey/green in colour with a grey mealy covering on the undersides. The narrow flower head, which appears in the late summer, is dense, grey and woolly. Individual flowers are tiny with green sepals and no petals.

COMMON MALLOW *Malva sylvestris*

The mallow family contains some very attractive plants with large mauve flowers. Common mallow, which is a perennial herb of dry waste ground and road verges, grows to nearly a metre in height and is one of the more impressive species. Its leaves are round or kidney shaped, lobed and shallowly toothed. The flowers grow in clusters from the leaf axils and are out from June to September. They are 3 or 4cm across, four petalled, mauve with darker lines, and have a central tube of stamens ending in a fuzzy pompom of anthers.

Marsh mallow, *Althaea officinalis*, a related coastal species, was once collected for its roots which were boiled up and made into sweets and herbal cures.

BROAD-LEAVED WILLOW-HERB

Epilobium montanum

Far less showy than either rosebay or the great willow-herb, this species is probably commoner than either in back gardens, urban wastes and in woodland. It is a perennial, flowering from June to August, spreading by stolons later in the year. The stem is usually 30—50cm tall, round in cross section, and bears opposite pairs of lance-shaped leaves. These are short stalked, finely toothed and broad only in comparison with other more willow-leaved species.

The flowers are 6—8mm across, pink with four notched petals and a four-lobed stigma. Like other willow-herbs the seeds are formed in long thin capsules which split to release them into the air on silky plumes.

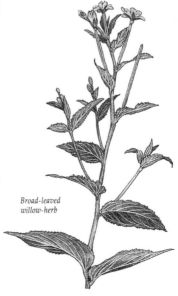

Broad-leaved willow-herb

ROSEBAY WILLOW-HERB

Chamaenerion angustifolium

Old books describe rosebay as a woodland plant, and so it still is, but it has become much more common in towns and cities, along railway lines and road verges. It thrives on the scorched ground left after bonfires and covered many bomb sites for years after World War II.

Were it as rare now as it was over a century ago rosebay would probably be more appreciated. It is a tall, very upright perennial often growing in dense stands to a height of over 120cm. The leaves are rather narrow, lance shaped with a finely toothed edge, and are arranged spirally up the smooth, red-flushed stem.

At the top of the stem is an impressive conical spike of flowers. These are up to 3cm across and have four purple sepals and four pink/purple petals, of which the upper pair are slightly notched and are broader than the lower pair. The stamens hang down in a gap between the lower petals, acting as a landing platform for pollinating insects. Once the pollen has gone the stamens shrivel and the stigma extends and opens into four thread-like styles, to receive pollen from other rosebay plants. The flowers are out from July to September, to be followed in the autumn by clouds of white-plumed seeds released from the slender four-sided capsules.

SUN SPURGE *Euphorbia helioscopia*

The poisonous white 'milk' exuded from spurges was once dabbed on to warts in a vague belief that it would burn or spirit them away.

Sun spurge is an annual weed of gardens and allotments, flowering from May to October. It grows to a height of 20 or 30cm, the single stem branching above five large leafy bracts into five rays. These bear alternate rounded leaves 2 or 3cm long, broadest and slightly serrated towards the tip. As in other spurges, the flowers (several male, one female) are tiny but are borne in a dish-shaped head of bracts containing four glands, like eggs in a nest. Viewed from above, the bright yellow-green bracts and rays are supposed to resemble a shining sun — hence the name.

HEMLOCK *Conium maculatum*
An evil reputation has followed hemlock around Europe for thousands of years; it contains a toxin, coniine, and has caused a few deliberate deaths, among which is listed that of the philosopher Socrates.

Hemlock is a member of the carrot family, a biennial growing to a height of 2m. The foliage is not so dense as in many other tall umbellifers. The leaves are delicate and fern like, about 30cm long but deeply divided, then divided again into small serrated leaflets. The umbrella-shaped flower heads are carried in a rather loose cluster of rays, with few bracts, and the individual flowers are only 2mm across, white and five petalled.

The slender, lacy appearance of the plant is a useful aid to identification. However, the best distinguishing features are hemlock's unpleasant smell (variously described as 'foetid' and 'mousey') and the presence of purple speckles all over the stem. Hemlock is found on waste ground and by ditches and rivers and is in flower during June and July. The skeletal remains of the stems and old seed heads last through the winter months.

JAPANESE KNOTWEED
Reynoutria japonica
This majestic Oriental import was contained within Victorian gardens for 100 years, but over the past 50 years it has become a nuisance along river banks, on rubbish dumps and in waste ground. The roots are spread in garden refuse and by flood water.

The reddish stems of Japanese knotweed grow to 2m tall, zig-zagging slightly between the alternate leaves. These leaves are the plant's most impressive feature, 10cm across, round but abruptly narrowing to a pointed tip. The flowers, out from August to October, are small and whitish, in narrow, 10cm-long spikes bushing outwards from the leaf axils.

BROAD-LEAVED DOCK

Rumex obtusifolius

Everyone who has been stung by a nettle looks for a dock leaf: the cooling effect of rubbing the sting with a smooth moist leaf certainly helps.

Broad-leaved dock is a notorious garden pest. It is a long-lived plant and has a deep rootstock, difficult to extract from a lawn without chemicals or a deep excavation. In ideal conditions the plant can grow a metre tall. The oval base leaves are about 30cm long, 10—15cm wide and have long stalks. The flowers are wind pollinated, so are small and without petals. They are gathered in whorls or tiers on tall branching stems, which also carry narrow, short-stalked leaves. In flower from June to October, broad-leaved dock prefers neutral, fertile soils. Gardens and urban wastes are therefore ideal.

STINGING NETTLE *Urtica dioica*

Stinging nettles grow profusely where fertile ground has been disturbed and where organic matter has enriched the soil with nitrogen and phosphorus. Thus patches of nettles are useful clues when looking for Victorian

rubbish dumps or other sites of buried treasure. In woodland — which is their true home — nettles and elders grow especially well on badger setts. In Africa and Asia, species of nettle grow 2 or 3m tall and carry a sting like a thunderbolt. Fortunately, our nettle only grows to a metre or so and the sting is relatively mild, though the formic acid (the same irritant as in ant stings) can cause a rash or 'urtication'. The best cure is a mild alkali such as bicarbonate of soda.

Stinging nettle is a perennial, creeping and rooting from the lower stems, and sending up ridged flowering shoots. These have opposite pairs of coarsely toothed, heart-shaped leaves. Male and female flowers are carried on different plants, in drooping tassels, but the plant is wind pollinated so the individual flowers are very small and green. They are out from June to September.

Nettle was once treated like flax and woven into a coarse country cloth for blankets. The fresh young leaves make an interesting green vegetable or soup, and nettle wine can be either an unexpected delight or a disaster. Altogether, a plant worthy of respect.

SCARLET PIMPERNEL *Anagallis arvensis*
Like its fictional namesake, the scarlet
pimpernel is likely to turn up anywhere; it is
also somewhat elusive for its flowers are only
open until early afternoon and then only if
the weather is fair. It is most common at the
edges of arable fields, where the stems trail
over the surface of the ground. They are up to
30cm long, square or oblong in cross section,
with opposite pairs of silky-smooth, dark-
green leaves, oval and without stalks.

The flowers arise singly on fine stalks
from the leaf axils. They are 10—14mm
across, with five green calyx teeth visible
between the five blunt corolla lobes. The
colour is very variable, but usually a clear
shade of red. Scarlet pimpernel is an annual,
flowering from June to August.

VERVAIN *Verbena officinalis*
A delicate flower of road verges and waste
places in southern England, vervain is
actually a tough perennial and the only
British representative of a tropical family that
includes the teak tree.

Although it grows up to 50cm tall it is a
remarkably inconspicuous plant. Its woody
rootstock sends up several tall stems with a
few pairs of opposite, deeply lobed leaves.
Slender spikes of short stalkless flowers arise
from the leaf axils and at the top of the main
stem. These flowers are small, only 4mm
across, with an attractive five-lobed corolla of
a dusty, pale-lilac colour. The flowers are out
from mid- to late summer. A modest plant
with no proven virtues, vervain was
venerated by the Romans and endowed with
mystical powers in medieval Britain.

LARGE BINDWEED *Calystegia sepium*
Gardeners have nightmares about bindweed;
its roots lurk deep in the ground and the
plant is almost impossible to eradicate.

Large bindweed is a climbing plant,
spiralling anti-clockwise up wire fences and
hedges to a height of 2 or 3m. The stem is
cord like, the leaves alternate, up to 15cm
long, heart shaped with a pointed tip and
with spreading lobes at the base. From June
to September the flowers make an impressive
show. The corolla is pure white, about 7cm
across, the shape of an ear trumpet,
narrowing to a five-lobed calyx enclosed in
leafy bracts.

COMMON TOADFLAX *Linaria vulgaris*
Once a weed of flax fields, toadflax is now more characteristic of road verges and waste ground on light soils. It is a perennial, sending up a simple stem which produces a spike of flowers in July. Later additional spikes from leaf axils are produced until by the autumn the plant is 70 or 80cm tall.

Common toadflax with detail of flower head

The leaves are very narrow, grouped in whorls on the lower stem but alternating towards the top. The flowers are up to 25mm long and have a long spur but are otherwise snapdragon shaped and bright yellow with an orange flush to the pouting lower lip or 'palate'. Bumblebees with long tongues, such as *Bombus hortorum*, are the pollinating agents, forcing their way into the flower and reaching into the spur at the back of the corolla where the nectar is stored.

RED DEAD-NETTLE *Lamium purpureum*
If some weeds are worse than others it follows that some must be better. Red dead-nettle is a universal inhabitant of gardens and allotments, yet it is pretty and easily removed if it becomes too obtrusive.

It is an annual, flowering through the summer and autumn, usually 10—20cm tall, with a hollow, square stem and opposite pairs of round or oval leaves. These are bluntly toothed, very hairy, and are dull green, often suffused with purple. From the upper leaf axils and bracts, whorls of flowers appear in dense groups of long five-toothed calyces and corollas. The pink/purple corolla is 10—15mm long, downy, tube shaped with a pinched throat, and separated into a hood above and a pair of lobes below.

The seeds, four little nutlets per calyx, have no obvious method of dispersal once they have fallen from the plant. In fact, they have an oily substance called an elaiosome attached to them which attracts ants, the insects carrying the nutlets far and wide.

WHITE DEAD-NETTLE *Lamium album*
White dead-nettle is a perennial, more robust than red dead-nettle but obviously closely related to it. It is also very similar to the yellow archangel (page 24) but is much more widespread, being found on waste ground and road verges throughout the country, from spring until the first hard frosts of winter.

The leaves are nettle-like, heart shaped and heavily toothed, but soft and downy and without a sting. The name 'dead-nettle' probably came from the old English term *deffe nettil*, which referred to a nettle that is disabled or powerless.

The flowers grow in whorls from leaf axils and bracts, often encircling the stem. They are about 3cm long, two-thirds of which is made up of the elegant white corolla. It detaches easily from the calyx. Dab the back on to your tongue and you can taste the nectar.

GREATER PLANTAIN *Plantago major*
As with red dead-nettle and a few other familiar weeds, this plant followed European settlers to the New World and was known to the American Indians as 'white man's foot'. It is a perennial of disturbed ground, forming a very low rosette, tolerant of trampling and

impossible to mow out of a lawn. The leaves are very broad and heavily veined, up to 15cm long, with a stalk of about the same length.

The flowers, which are wind pollinated, are tiny — only 2 or 3mm long — with a cream-coloured, four-lobed corolla, long stigmas and styles. They are carried in a long narrow spike 20cm or more tall; just the right size, shape and colour to have earned the plant its alternative English name of rat's tail plantain.

CLEAVERS *Galium aparine*
The hooked bristles on the stem and fruits of cleavers ensure that it is efficiently dispersed. It is an annual herb of hedgerows and waste ground, sprawling among more robust vegetation to a height of up to a metre. The leaves are narrow, in whorls of 6—8 at a time. The flowers are tiny, four-lobed and whitish, in clusters from the leaf axils.

The well-known 'sticky-willie' fruits, round and about 5mm across, are found from mid- to late summer, mostly clinging to people's socks.

Cleavers

OXFORD RAGWORT *Senecio squalidus*

A plant associated with railway lines, crumbling walls and back-street rubble, Oxford ragwort was brought over from Italy in the 17th century and planted in the Oxford Botanic Garden. It made its escape in the following century and is still on the increase, but it adds such a splash of colour to drab inner cities that it is more of a street decoration than a weed.

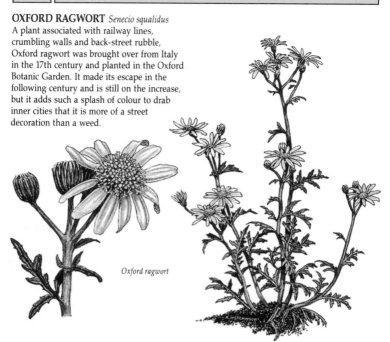

Oxford ragwort

Oxford ragwort is an annual, growing to a height of 20—30cm. The leaves are deeply fingered with a few broad teeth near the tips of the lobes. Those at the base of the plant are stalked and less deeply indented, those high on the stem are stalkless and more skeletal. The daisy-like flower heads are out from May to early winter and are carried in a broad, branching terminal bunch or inflorescence. They are up to 20cm across and have bright-yellow disc and ray florets. Underneath the platform of florets there is a ring of green bracts with distinctive black-tipped teeth.

Common ragwort, *Senecio jacobaea*, is a closely related native species of neglected pastures. It has much more complex, ragged leaves (which are often stripped by cinnabar moth caterpillars) and can become a serious problem because the plant is poisonous to grazing animals.

GROUNDSEL *Senecio vulgaris*

Groundsel is an unobtrusive annual weed, flowering all year long and found virtually everywhere. Its only real claim to fame is as a midwinter food supplement for family pets such as rabbits and canaries.

The plant usually grows 15—25cm tall, a single stem at first with a tight cluster of flowers at the tip, but through the summer and autumn the plant branches and the heads space out to give themselves room to seed. The leaves are deeply divided into 2 or 3 pairs of spiky lobes. The flower heads are about a centimetre long, tubular with smooth green bracts topped by a tuft of yellow disc florets. though as in most of the daisy family there is some variation; you can find ragwort without ray florets and groundsel with them.

The name for the genus comes from the Latin *senex*, an old man, referring to the untidy, drooping, white-haired seed heads.

COLTSFOOT *Tussilago farfara*

For commuters, the brilliant yellow glow of coltsfoot flowers on bare railway banks and verges offers a real hint of spring. The plant puts most of its food reserves into the flush of flowers; the leaves come later and spend the summer photosynthesising to replenish the rootstock and runners with energy for the following spring.

The flower heads are carried singly on thick, woolly, scaly stems 10—15cm tall, and are composed of a great number of narrow female ray florets and a much smaller group of male disc florets. The heads are 20—30mm across. When they have finished flowering in March and April they droop and elongate, then raise themselves again to release the seeds which are wind dispersed by parachute (or 'pappus'). The leaves always come after the flowers. They are cobwebby and plate sized with an angled edge so that they look

polygonal. When they are fully developed they are smooth and green on the top but with thick white felt underneath.

During World War II the leaves were collected and dried, then chopped up and mixed with tobacco to bolster the country's cigarette reserves.

DAISY *Bellis perennis*

We take the little perennial daisy for granted. It brightens many a dull council lawn even after cutting. The rosette of downy, slightly toothed, spoon-shaped leaves are so low growing that they avoid the mower blades.

The flower heads, rising singly from downy stems, are not so fortunate but are quickly replaced and continue to be produced throughout the year. They are 15—25mm across, composed of a plate of yellow disc florets and a fringe of petal-like ray florets, white with a red tip.

The flower head is a composition of florets and the florets are a composition of stamens and stigmas; hence the title for the whole daisy/dandelion family, the *Compositae*. The daisy closes at night, which is how it came by its modest name, 'day's eye'.

PINEAPPLE MAYWEED *Matricaria matricarioides*

This plant has spread worldwide from North-East Asia, reaching Britain via North America in about 1870. Its seeds do not have parachutes and rely for dispersal on muddy rainwater. The unsurfaced roads of the 1900s were very muddy and cars managed in a few years what nature might have taken centuries to achieve.

Pineapple or rayless mayweed is a daisy without petals; it has no ray florets but a dense conical head of yellow disc florets 5—8mm across. Two or three heads are produced from each of the upper axils in June and July. An annual weed of disturbed ground, especially farm tracks and gateways, it grows 3—30cm tall and has smooth alternate leaves. These are broad based and divided into lobes which are themselves deeply divided so that the foliage seems very feathery. Roll a flower head between your fingers and it will give off a remarkably good imitation of pineapple's sharp, acid scent.

MUGWORT *Artemesia vulgaris*

Mugwort was hung up in cottages to keep ghosts away and was kept as a charm by travellers. It is still a common roadside herb and forms part of the general swathe of tall foliage covering demolition sites and urban wastes. The stem grows to a height of over a metre and is grooved and reddish in colour.

The leaves are alternate, 6 or 7cm long, deeply divided and lobed, and are dark green above and silky white below. The flower heads are carried in a dense woolly spike at the top of the stem and on shorter clusters growing from the upper leaf axils. They are 2 or 3mm across, composed of brown florets which are wind pollinated, and are out from June to September.

Both mugwort and its close relative **wormwood**, *A. absinthium*, are aromatic and are widely used in folk medicine. Wormwood is a slightly shorter plant, with leaves silvery on both sides, and with less woolly, yellow-topped flower heads. It was used as a cure for internal worms and is the source of absinthe, a fierce French liquor.

FEVERFEW *Tanacetum parthenium*
Many familiar wild herbs were introduced
into cottage gardens hundreds of years ago
and are still only found a stone's throw from
habitation. Writing in the early 17th century,
the great herbalist Gerard found feverfew 'in
hedges, gardens, and about old wals' where
'it joyeth to grow among rubbish'.

The aromatic herb had earned its place
close to the home because of its medicinal
qualities, in particular as a cure for dizziness
and headaches. The name 'ferverfew' is a
corruption of 'febrifuge' meaning a cure for
fever, and it was used as a family stand-by in
much the same way as aspirin.

Feverfew is a bushy perennial flowering
from July to September. The leaves are deeply
divided into lobed segments and are yellow/
green and downy. When crushed or rubbed
they certainly have a refreshing quality,
perhaps enough to cure a thick head. The
branching stem grows to a height of about
50cm and is topped by an umbrella-shaped
platform of flower heads. These measure
15—20mm across with short, broad, white ray
florets encircling a bright-yellow button of
disc florets.

LESSER BURDOCK *Arctium minus*
Throwing the sticky hooked burrs of burdock
into people's hair or on to their backs was one
of the pleasures of an unsophisticated
childhood. Lesser burdock is a plant of
hedgerows and waste places and is a biennial
growing 1—2m tall. The stem is thick, downy
and branched, and the rhubarb-shaped leaves
are up to 40cm long. These are also downy
and have a characteristic smell, nostalgic for
those who can remember the original
dandelion and burdock pop.

The flower heads resemble those of
thistles, tufts of red/purple florets just visible
within an enclosing tube of spiky, hooked
bracts. They are out from July to September
but the burrs and the skeletal remains of the
plant persist for months afterwards. The more
local **greater burdock**, *A. lappa*, is similar but
has even broader, heart-shaped leaves (as
wide as they are long) and larger flower
heads (3—4cm rather than 2—3cm).

*Lesser burdock
with detail of
flower head*

SPEAR THISTLE *Cirsium vulgare*
A majestic biennial of pastures, verges and waste ground, spear thistle overwinters as a prickly rosette of leaves, then sends up a straight stem over a metre tall which produces flowers from July to October of its second year.

It has sharp spines everywhere: on ridges all the way up the cottony stem, on the lobed, spear-shaped leaves, and on the bracts that cover the egg-shaped flower heads. The flower heads are 2—3cm across, composed of an outer mesh of spiny bracts and an inner core of florets with a protruding tuft of pink/purple corollas. After flowering, the heads open to release the fruits. These are dispersed on the slightest breeze by a feathery white pappus or parachute of plumes.

CREEPING THISTLE *Cirsium arvense*
Although not one of the most impressive of thistles this is probably the most troublesome to farmers. It is a perennial, radiating surface roots which then send up new flowering shoots, so that whole pastures deteriorate and have to be cut or sprayed with herbicides.

The stem grows 50—80cm tall. The leaves are lance shaped, divided into spine-bearing lobes, with no obvious rosette at the base. The flower heads appear from July to September. They are about a centimetre across with a covering of purple, short-spined bracts and a large tuft of purple/mauve florets. Male and female flowers grow on different plants, the male flower head being round whilst the female flower head is more oval or egg shaped.

DANDELION *Taraxacum spp.*
Dandelions are more complicated than they look. There are actually 200 different 'microspecies' and it is best to talk about them as an 'aggregate' rather than to try to describe any particular one.

Dandelions grow from milky tap roots and develop rosettes of lance-shaped radical leaves, sharply lobed and broadening towards the tip. From the heart of the rosette grow several leafless hollow stalks each of which produces a flower head usually 3—5cm across. This is composed of two rows of green bracts and a head of bright-yellow florets. The young leaves are good in salads and the roots have been roasted as a coffee substitute. Dandelions have medicinal virtues too, notably in laxatives and diuretics.

FURTHER READING

Flowers may be a simple pleasure but choosing flower books is quite different.

If this is the first book in your flower library your next step will be to buy a more complete field guide. *The Wild Flowers of Britain and Northern Europe* by Fitter, Fitter and Blamey and published by Collins, has been the standard pocket guide since it was first published in 1974, but *The Wild Flower Key* by Francis Rose, first published by Warne in 1981, is an excellent and more scientific alternative. Both of these books are illustrated in colour though the quality is variable and it is a good idea to look out for a copy of the beautifully illustrated *Wild Flowers of the British Isles* by Garrard and Streeter (published by Macmillan in 1983) to keep for reference at home. To solve obscure identification problems, the most authoritative book about wild flowers is the classic *Flora of the British Isles* by Clapham, Tutin and Warburg. This runs to hundreds of pages of condensed text and is a gold mine or a minefield depending on your level of competence and confidence.

Finally, there must be a place on the bookshelf for magical, well-written books about finding and enjoying flowers. Of these, *The Flowering of Britain* by Richard Mabey (Hutchinson 1980) is without equal.

A NOTE ABOUT NAMES

Linnaeus, who devised the modern scientific system for naming plants and animals, might have been perplexed at the speed with which immutable names seem to change. There are good reasons for the continuing revision of plant families and genera, but this hardly helps when you are trying to chase a plant identification from one book to another. The common names in this book are those in general use and are thus taken from a variety of sources. The scientific names follow Garrard and Streeter's *Wild Flowers of the British Isles* (Macmillan 1983).

SOCIETIES

Joining clubs and societies is a matter of personal taste and commitment, but anyone concerned about their local wildlife should at least be a member of their local Nature Conservation Trust, which manages nature reserves and organises meetings to raise funds for local conservation projects. Most cities, and many towns and villages, have Natural History Societies or Field Clubs which hold regular talks and field visits and sometimes organise surveys. Find their addresses from your local library. Such groups may seem fuddy-duddy or a little eccentric but in fact they are often very lively and are the descendants of organisations which sprang up early this century to revitalise the great tradition of amateur natural history in this country.

There are also urban wildlife groups whose addresses can again be found in local libraries. Continued vitality depends upon fresh ideas and enthusiasm from each new generation. For children, there are **WATCH** groups, further details of which can be obtained from *22 The Green, Nettleham, Lincoln LN2 2NR.*

Two national societies are worthy of note. These are the **Wild Flower Society,** at *Rams Hill House, Horsemonden, Tonbridge, Kent,* and the **Botanic Society of the British Isles,** *c/o The Natural History Museum, Cromwell Road, London SW7* (prospective members should write to these addresses). The former is for the true amateur, the latter a more serious organisation but with a marvellously lively newsletter and an excellent programme of field trips. If this book has stimulated your interest in wild flowers, it is well worth joining either — or both — of these societies.

GLOSSARY

Achene Dry, one-seeded fruit.

Aggregate Collection of species of plant that look almost identical. They are separated by small physiological differences.

Anther The part of the stamen that produces pollen.

Axil; Leaf axil The angle between the leaf stalk and the stem. It contains axillary buds or shoots.

Base-rich A soil rich in lime; pH greater than 7.

Basal leaves Leaves at the base of the stem at soil level.

Basic soil See Base-rich.

Biennial A plant that takes two years to complete its life cycle.

Bract A small modified leaf with a flower or branch of flowers in its axil.

Calcareous Lime-rich.

Calcicole Grows best on calcareous soils.

Calyx The outermost part of a flower, made up of sepals, protecting the flower when in bud. Separate parts can join forming a calyx tube.

Capsule Dry fruit case with many compartments. Opens to shake out dry, ripe seeds.

Carpel Stigma-topped ovary containing ovules which, after fertilisation, become the seeds.

Chlorophyll The green pigment in plants.

Coppicing The practice of cropping strong, thin poles from the bases of trees in a rotation basis.

Corolla The petals of a flower.

Corymb Flowers arranged alternately on opposite sides of the stem, the outer, lower flower stalks being longer than the inner, higher ones. This gives flowers a flat-topped cluster.

Cruciform Cross shaped. All crucifer flowers are typically cross shaped.

Disc florets Petal tubes containing stamens and a stigma with an ovary in the base. A complete mini-flower. Characteristic of the button centre of daisies.

Downland Type of grassland associated with chalk soils.

Drupe Any fruit that has a fleshy part around a stone that encloses a seed (eg peach).

Dune slack The gap between and behind sand dunes.

Emergent plants Plants with stems and leaves rising up out of the water.

Ephemeral A plant with a short life cycle.

Filament The stem of a stamen.

Flower spike An unbranched stalk of flowers without individual stalks.

Herb Non-woody plant that dies back each winter to an underground tuber or rhizome, or to a basal leaf rosette.

Inflorescence All flowering parts of the plant including buds and forming seeds. These may take many forms, eg raceme, umbel, corymb, spike, spadix, panicle.

Involucre A group of bracts protecting the young inflorescence in composites.

Lime-deficient Acidic soils; soils lacking in lime; pH of less than 7.

Nectar Sugary substance manufactured in the nectary. Attractive to insects.

Node The point at which a leaf is joined to the stem.

Nutlets Type of fruit/seed, especially in dead-nettles.

Ovule Female part of the plant, inside the carpel. Develops into a seed after fertilisation.

Panicle Flowers arranged in small branches in a raceme.

Perennial Plants that grow from year to year.

Perianth Outer part of the flower that encloses stamens and carpels.

Raceme An elongated arrangement of flowers up the stem, where the lowest opens first and those of the tip last.

Radical leaves Leaves that grow from the root of the plant.

Ray floret Strap-shaped mini-flower containing stamens and stigma with an ovary at its base. Characteristic of outer 'petals' of a daisy.

Rhizome Thick underground stem, bearing leaf scars.

Saltings The margins of tidal land, subject to saline flooding.

Self-pollination Flowers whose stigmas receive their own pollen, or that of another flower on the same plant.

Semi-parasitic Green plant capable of making its own food but needing some of its nutrients from the host plant. Penetrates the host plant with its roots.

Sepals Leaf-like parts of a flower which cover the bud and surround the petals. Usually green.

Spadix A bract enclosing the inflorescence of flowers such as cuckoo-pint.

Stamen The male organ of the flower that produces pollen.

Stile A stem-like structure of the carpel that holds up the stigma.

Tendril Thread-like part of a plant that twines around other structures.

Trifoliate Leaves cut into three parts like clover.

Umbel Flower in a flat-topped cluster, the stalks of which all arise from one point at the top of the stem.

Whorl Ring of leaves.

INDEX
(Page references to colour photographs/illustrations appear in **bold**.)

A
agrimony 41, **45**
  hemp 84
Alexanders 85, 97
anemone, wood 13, **25**
archangel, yellow 24, **26**
asphodel, bog 70
aster, sea 100
avens, wood 18

B
bacon-and-eggs 39
balsam
  Himalayan **66**, 75
  orange 75
bedstraw
  heath 69
  lady's 50
beet, sea 92
bellflower, giant **26**, 29
bilberry 61
bindweed, large 109
bird's eye 43
bistort, amphibious 78
bittersweet **48**, 79
blackberry 17
blood-drop-emlets 80
bluebell **26**, 31
  Scottish 69
bogbean **67**, 79
brandy bottles 73
brooklime 81
broom 58
bryony, white 21
bugle 29
bugloss, vipers **68**, 99
burdock
  greater 115
  lesser 115
Burnet, salad 40
butterbur 84
buttercup
  bulbous **27**, 34
  creeping 102
  meadow 34
butterwort 64

C
cabbage, wild 92
campion
  moss **48**, 57
  red 14, **25**
  sea 68, 94
celandine, lesser 14, **25**
centaury, common 43
charlock 103
chickweed **86**, 104
Cicely, sweet 42
cleavers 111
clover
  Dutch 37
  red **28**, 38
  white 37
coltsfoot 113
comfrey 83
cowberry **48**, 60
cowslip 44
cow-wheat, common 23
cranberry 62
crane's-bill, meadow **27**, 37
crosswort 50
crowberry 60
cuckoo flower **48**, 74
cuckoo-pint 32

D
daffodil, wild 32
daisy **88**, 113
  moon 52
  ox eye **46**, 52
dandelion 116
day's eye 113
dead-nettle
  red **87**, 110
  white **88**, 111
dock
  broad-leaved 108
  great water 78
dodder 63
dog's mercury 20

E
everlasting, mountain **47**, 69
eyebright, common 44, **46**

F
fat hen 105
feverfew 115
figwort
  common 22
  water 80
forget-me-not
  creeping 83
  water 83
  wood 23
foxglove 22, **27**
fumitory **86**, 103

G
garlic
  hedge 15
  mustard 15
gipsywort **65**, 82
glasswort 95
globe flower 13
goat's-beard 52
Goldilocks 13
gorse 58
  dwarf 95
  western 95
groundsel **88**

H
hard head 53
harebell **48**, 69
hawkbit
  autumn 70
  rough 70
hawkweed 53
heartsease **86**, 104
heath, cross-leaved **46**, 62
heather 61
  bell 62
hemlock 107
herb Bennet 18

herb Robert 16, **25**
hogweed
  common 42 **67**,
  giant 76
holly, sea 85, 97
honeysuckle 30

I
iris, yellow 90
ivy, ground-24, **28**

J
Jack-by-the-hedge 15, **25**
Jack-go-to-bed-at-noon 52

K
knapweed
  black 53
  common 53
  greater 53
knotweed, Japanese 107

L
lady's mantle 41
  alpine 56
lady smock 74
ling 61
loosestrife
  purple **67**, 78
  yellow 79
lords and ladies 32
lousewort **48**, 64
  marsh 64

M
mallow
  common 105
  marsh 105
mare's-tail **66**, 73
marguerite 52
marigold, marsh 13, **65**, 72
mayweed
  pineapple 114
  rayless 114

meadowsweet 75
mignonette 104
milfoil 51
milkwort
    common **28**, 35
    heath **47**, 57
    sea **68**, 99
mint, water 81
Molly blobs 72
monkey flower **67**, 80
mouse-ear, common 36
mugwort 114

N

nettle, stinging 108
nightshade, enchanter's 19

O

orache, frosted **66**, 94
orchid
    common spotted **47**, 54
    early purple **46**, 54
    heath spotted **65**, 70
    northern marsh **68**, 90
    southern marsh 90

P

pansy
    mountain **47**, 56
    wild 104
parsley, cow 42, **45**
pennywort
    marsh 77
    wall 77
pignut 42, **45**
pimpernel
    scarlet **87**, 109
    yellow 21
pink, maiden **27**, 36
plantain
    greater **87**, 111
    rat's tail 111
    ribwort 49
    water 90
poppy
    common **86**, 102
    field 102
    long-headed 102
    prickly 102
    yellow-horned **68**, 92
primrose 21, **26**

Q

Queen Anne's lace 42

R

ragged robin **66**, 75
ragwort
    common 112
    Oxford **88**, 112
ramsons **27**, 31

rattle
    corn 49
    hay 49
    yellow **46**, 49
rest harrow 38
rocket
    dyer's 104
    sea 93
rockrose, common 35
rose
    Burnet **85**, 96
    dog 19, **26**
    downy 19

S

St John's wort
    perforate 35
    trailing 57
salsify 52
saltwort, black 99
samphire, rock 97
sandwort, sea **85**, 94
sanicle 20
saxifrage
    alternate-leaved golden 76
    opposite-leaved golden 76
scabious
    devil's bit 51
    field 51
    small 51
scurvy grass 93
sea lavender 98
    lax-flowered 98
selfheal **46**, 49
shepherd's purse 103
silverweed **28**, 40
skullcap 82
sneezewort **66**, 89
snow-in-summer 36
sorrel
    common 42
    wood 15
spearwort, lesser 72
speedwell
    germander 43, **45**
    heath 63
spurge
    sea 98
    sun 106
squill
    autumn 100
    spring **86**, 100
stitchwort, greater 16
stonecrop
    biting 96
    English 96
stork's-bill **67**, 95
strawberry
    barren 19, **26**
    cultivated 18
    wild 18
sundew, round-leaved 59

T

thistle
    carline **85**, 100
    creeping **88**, 116
    marsh 89
    spear 116
thousand-leaf 51
thrift **85**, 99
thyme
    garden 44
    large 44
    wild 44, **45**
toadflax, common **87**, 110
tormentil 59
touch-me-not 75
trefoil, bird's-foot 39

V

valerian **68**, 83
vervain 109
vetch
    horseshoe 38
    kidney **28**, 39
    tufted 17
violet
    common dog 14
    marsh **47**, 56
    pale dog 14
    sweet 14

W

wallpepper 96
water-cress 74
water crowfoot,
    common **65**, 72
water-dropwort, hemlock 77
water-lily
    white 73
    yellow **65**, 73
welcome-home-husband-
    though-never-so-drunk 96
weld 104
willow-herb
    broad-leaved **86**, 105
    great **66**, 76
    rosebay **87**, 106
winter-cress 74
woodruff 30
wormwood 114
woundwort, hedge 24

Y

yarrow 51